FRANCIS FRITH'S

FALKIRK - A HISTORY & CELEBRATION

THE FRANCIS FRITH COLLECTION

www.francisfrith.com

FALKIRK

A HISTORY & CELEBRATION

DAVID ELLIOT

THE FRANCIS FRITH COLLECTION

www.francisfrith.com

First published in the United Kingdom in 2005
by The Francis Frith Collection®

Hardback edition 2005 ISBN 1-84589-202-X
Paperback edition 2012 ISBN 978-1-84589-700-0

Text and Design copyright © The Francis Frith Collection®
Photographs copyright © The Francis Frith Collection®
except where indicated

The Frith® photographs and the Frith® logo are reproduced under
licence from Heritage Photographic Resources Ltd, the owners of the
Frith® archive and trademarks
'The Francis Frith Collection', 'Francis Frith' and 'Frith' are registered
trademarks of Heritage Photographic Resources Ltd.

British Library Cataloguing in Publication Data

Falkirk - A History & Celebration
David Elliot

The Francis Frith Collection®
Oakley Business Park, Wylye Road,
Dinton, Wiltshire SP3 5EU
Tel: +44 (0) 1722 716 376
Email: info@francisfrith.co.uk
www.francisfrith.com

Printed and bound in Great Britain
Contains material sourced from responsibly managed forests

Front Cover: **FALKIRK, A TRAMCAR IN THE HIGH STREET**
c1910 ZZZ05067t (Falkirk Council Cultural Services/Falkirk Herald)

Additional modern photographs by David Elliot, Elspeth Reid and
Alexander Burt unless otherwise specified.
Domesday extract used in timeline by kind permission of
Alecto Historical Editions, www.domesdaybook.org
Aerial photographs reproduced under licence from
Simmons Aerofilms Limited.
Historical Ordnance Survey maps reproduced under licence from
Homecheck.co.uk

Every attempt has been made to contact copyright holders of
illustrative material. We will be happy to give full acknowledgement in
future editions for any items not credited. Any information should be
directed to The Francis Frith Collection.

*The colour-tinting in this book is for illustrative purposes only,
and is not intended to be historically accurate*

AS WITH ANY HISTORICAL DATABASE, THE FRANCIS FRITH ARCHIVE IS
CONSTANTLY BEING CORRECTED AND IMPROVED, AND THE PUBLISHERS
WOULD WELCOME INFORMATION ON OMISSIONS OR INACCURACIES

CONTENTS

FALKIRK FROM THE AIR 1969 AFA197574

A HISTORY & CELEBRATION

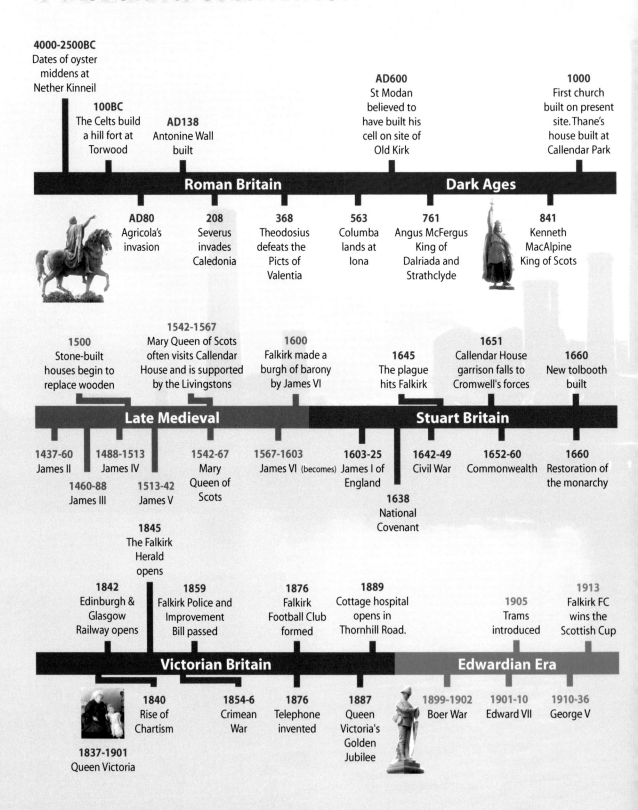

4000-2500BC
Dates of oyster middens at Nether Kinneil

100BC
The Celts build a hill fort at Torwood

AD138
Antonine Wall built

AD600
St Modan believed to have built his cell on site of Old Kirk

1000
First church built on present site. Thane's house built at Callendar Park

Roman Britain

Dark Ages

AD80
Agricola's invasion

208
Severus invades Caledonia

368
Theodosius defeats the Picts of Valentia

563
Columba lands at Iona

761
Angus McFergus King of Dalriada and Strathclyde

841
Kenneth MacAlpine King of Scots

1500
Stone-built houses begin to replace wooden

1542-1567
Mary Queen of Scots often visits Callendar House and is supported by the Livingstons

1600
Falkirk made a burgh of barony by James VI

1645
The plague hits Falkirk

1651
Callendar House garrison falls to Cromwell's forces

1660
New tolbooth built

Late Medieval

Stuart Britain

1437-60
James II

1488-1513
James IV

1460-88
James III

1513-42
James V

1542-67
Mary Queen of Scots

1567-1603
James VI (becomes)

1603-25
James I of England

1638
National Covenant

1642-49
Civil War

1652-60
Commonwealth

1660
Restoration of the monarchy

1845
The Falkirk Herald opens

1842
Edinburgh & Glasgow Railway opens

1859
Falkirk Police and Improvement Bill passed

1876
Falkirk Football Club formed

1889
Cottage hospital opens in Thornhill Road.

1905
Trams introduced

1913
Falkirk FC wins the Scottish Cup

Victorian Britain

Edwardian Era

1840
Rise of Chartism

1854-6
Crimean War

1876
Telephone invented

1887
Queen Victoria's Golden Jubilee

1899-1902
Boer War

1901-10
Edward VII

1910-36
George V

1837-1901
Queen Victoria

HISTORICAL TIMELINE FOR FALKIRK

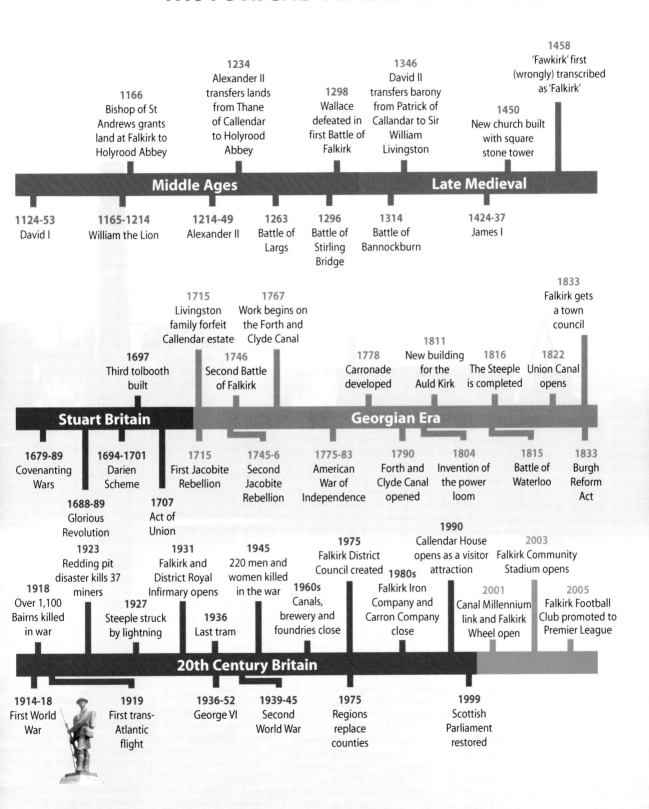

1166
Bishop of St Andrews grants land at Falkirk to Holyrood Abbey

1234
Alexander II transfers lands from Thane of Callendar to Holyrood Abbey

1298
Wallace defeated in first Battle of Falkirk

1346
David II transfers barony from Patrick of Callandar to Sir William Livingston

1450
New church built with square stone tower

1458
'Fawkirk' first (wrongly) transcribed as 'Falkirk'

Middle Ages   ## Late Medieval

1124-53
David I

1165-1214
William the Lion

1214-49
Alexander II

1263
Battle of Largs

1296
Battle of Stirling Bridge

1314
Battle of Bannockburn

1424-37
James I

1715
Livingston family forfeit Callendar estate

1767
Work begins on the Forth and Clyde Canal

1833
Falkirk gets a town council

1697
Third tolbooth built

1746
Second Battle of Falkirk

1778
Carronade developed

1811
New building for the Auld Kirk

1816
The Steeple is completed

1822
Union Canal opens

Stuart Britain   ## Georgian Era

1679-89
Covenanting Wars

1694-1701
Darien Scheme

1715
First Jacobite Rebellion

1745-6
Second Jacobite Rebellion

1775-83
American War of Independence

1790
Forth and Clyde Canal opened

1804
Invention of the power loom

1815
Battle of Waterloo

1833
Burgh Reform Act

1688-89
Glorious Revolution

1707
Act of Union

1923
Redding pit disaster kills 37 miners

1931
Falkirk and District Royal Infirmary opens

1945
220 men and women killed in the war

1975
Falkirk District Council created

1980s
Falkirk Iron Company and Carron Company close

1990
Callendar House opens as a visitor attraction

2003
Falkirk Community Stadium opens

1918
Over 1,100 Bairns killed in war

1927
Steeple struck by lightning

1936
Last tram

1960s
Canals, brewery and foundries close

2001
Canal Millennium link and Falkirk Wheel open

2005
Falkirk Football Club promoted to Premier League

20th Century Britain

1914-18
First World War

1919
First trans-Atlantic flight

1936-52
George VI

1939-45
Second World War

1975
Regions replace counties

1999
Scottish Parliament restored

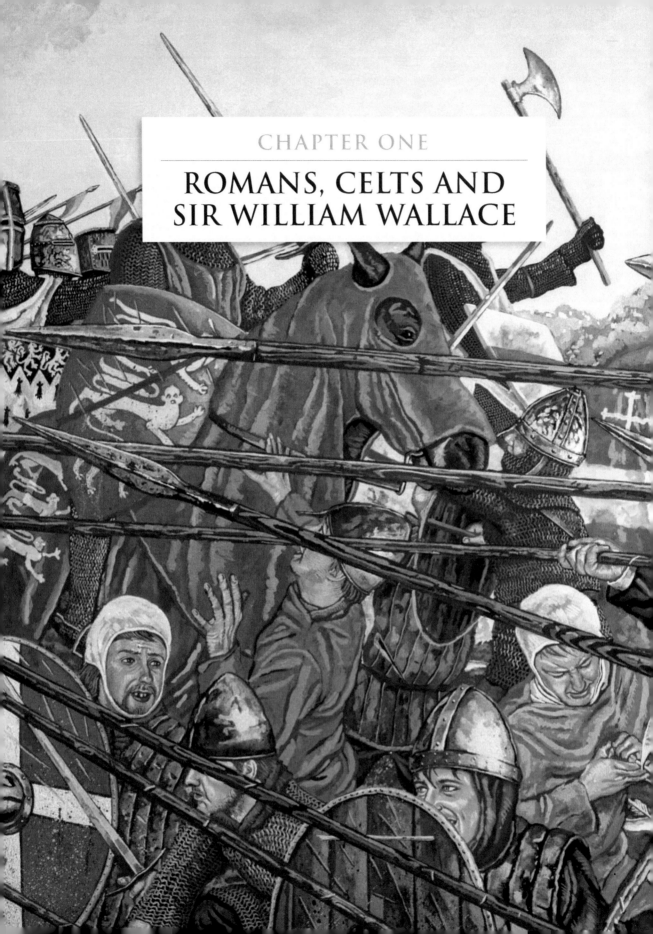

CHAPTER ONE

ROMANS, CELTS AND SIR WILLIAM WALLACE

FALKIRK'S POWERFUL SENSE of identity is summed up, not in some obscure Latin motto, but in robust Scots: 'Ane for a: better meddle wi the deil than the Bairns o Falkirk'. Perhaps this identity comes from the town lying in the heart of Scotland, between the heights of Falkirk Muir to the south and the flat carse lands to the north. The Romans quickly recognised the importance of the location. They built a huge fort at Camelon and, later, a defensive wall along what was to become the site of the town. In the centuries of the Scottish monarchy, the road between the royal burghs of Edinburgh, Linlithgow and Stirling passed through Falkirk. In more modern times the networks of canals, toll roads, rail lines and motorways all confirm the town's central position. In 1995 Falkirk finally achieved county town status, for an area which stretches from the Campsie Fells in the west to the ancient castle of Blackness in the east.

This sense of identity has also come out of adversity. Falkirk Bairns have witnessed several bloody battles on their doorstep and the comings and goings of famous national figures such as Sir William Wallace, Mary Queen of Scots and Bonnie Prince Charlie. In the 18th and especially the 19th century, Falkirk was a major player in an industrial revolution that swept the land. Some citizens enjoyed great material rewards, but many laboured long and hard in living and working conditions that were desperate. Perhaps out of these historical struggles has come that sense of common purpose summed up in 'ane for a'. Falkirk's story is both long and dramatic and the physical traces of much of

it are still around us today.

We know little about the first inhabitants. They came after the ice sheet retreated northwards some 10,000 years ago. It was the glaciers flowing from the southwest towards the River Forth that dumped the boulders, sand and clay, many metres deep, on which most of the town is built. As the climate warmed, oak, elm and ash trees grew and the woods filled with beavers, bears, roe deer, wolves, boar and wild cattle. On the upland muirs, amongst the birch, rowan and pine were grouse, blackcock and capercaillie. The rivers and seas were rich with fish and shellfish. Not quite a land of milk and honey, but food in abundance for these early hunters and gatherers.

The ridge along which the High Street runs today was adopted as a place to settle. It was high enough to be well drained, when most low-lying ground was boggy. The ridge would have given some protection from unwelcome guests. To the north lay the low-lying carse, stretching to the Forth.

These first inhabitants came across the North Sea, hugging the coasts in dug-out canoes or coracles. Some came overland. They probably already knew about herding animals, but their greatest challenge was making clearings in the forest. Cutting down a tree with a modern handsaw is hard work; doing it with a blade of flint was gruelling. Flint is a hard rock which takes a sharp edge when chipped. It is found in limestone of which there is little in Scotland, so it was probably imported: trading over long distances goes back to the earliest times.

Evidence of how these early folk lived is still buried in the soil beneath our feet. Archaeologists have already found middens or dumps of oyster shells, for example 15 tonnes of them at Nether Kinneil dating from 4000 to 2500 BC. What is now a luxury was a staple diet. Sharp-eyed individuals have found a harpoon made of antler on the shore of the Forth, an arrowhead at Brightons, a fragment of bronze spearhead at Dalderse, and a bronze axe head at Carriden. A stone kist at Camelon contained cremated remains, food vessels and flint tools from around 1500 BC.

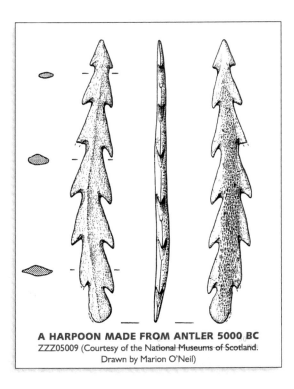

A HARPOON MADE FROM ANTLER 5000 BC
ZZZ05009 (Courtesy of the National Museums of Scotland.
Drawn by Marion O'Neil)

We know more about a later wave of immigrants, the Celts, who arrived in numbers around 100 BC and built a hill fort at Torwood. They had iron tools and were expert in the use of horses. Rather than relying totally on fishing and hunting they grew crops and kept animals. They wore furs and woollen clothing fastened with buttons.

THE TAPPOCH BROCH

The hill fort at Torwood, north of Larbert, is a broch. Most brochs are in the north and west of Scotland so Falkirk is unusual in having one in the area. It sits on top of Tappoch Hill, above a steep drop. From its walls you can see the castle rock of Stirling to the north and Falkirk to the south. The walls were once about seven metres high and six metres thick at the base. The space inside is about ten metres wide. Brochs were built with walls of wood and stone.

THE TAPPOCH BROCH 2005
ZZZ05010 (David Elliot)

Celts elsewhere had been fighting the Roman Empire for a while, but it must still have been a chilling sight when the army of imperial Rome first appeared in their midst. The men marched in columns, dressed in uniforms of steel helmets, shoulder plates and chain mail, and equipped with sword, dagger, javelin and shield. Above the troops fluttered the red banner and imperial eagle of Rome. When the troops halted, they quickly organised into work parties to build a fortified camp. When not on the move or engaged in fighting, they trained to fight. Food and other supplies were brought to them over great distances.

The Roman empire was vast, extending to the Rhine and the Danube. For 25 years the Falkirk area lay on the northern border; the southern border was level with Tenerife. The Caledonians did not meekly accept Roman rule and constantly attacked the line of forts. But the Romans had what the Celts lacked - organisation and a disciplined fighting force. In AD 83 their governor Agricola led a march north through the Falkirk area laying waste to the countryside and defeating the Celts at Mons Graupius. The leader of the Caledonians, Calgacus, said 'They make a desert, and call it peace'.

In AD 138, Antoninus Pius decided to build a wall along this northerly frontier. It required 9,000 men, drawn from Spain, France, the Rhine and Syria. At Callendar Park the wall crossed someone's arable field and it even cut through houses. Just like the Berlin Wall or the wall on the West Bank, members of families found themselves living on either side of it. Part of a settlement at Falkirk was levelled for the fort.

Work on the wall began from the main road north at Watling Lodge and proceeded westwards. A road was built to allow men and materials to be moved easily into position.

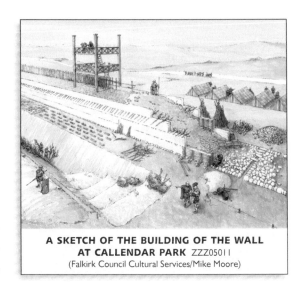

A SKETCH OF THE BUILDING OF THE WALL AT CALLENDAR PARK ZZZ05011
(Falkirk Council Cultural Services/Mike Moore)

Kerbstones for the edges of the wall base were dressed on the spot and placed in position. The rest of the base was then filled with stones and boulders. Streams which crossed the wall were forced through stone culverts, for example over the West Burn. Turfs were cut from a huge area and used like bricks to build the wall. (A turf-cutting tool has been found at Camelon.) Timber for the defences and the buildings was cut using iron axes and saws. The eastern section of the frontier was protected by the Firth of Forth, and so was built last. That section was made of earth piled between two narrow clay walls.

The wall was a fearsome obstacle for approaching warriors. First they had to scramble up a banking, exposed on its flattened top to the soldiers on the watchtowers or along the wall. They then had to slither down into a V-shaped ditch, about 12 metres wide and four and a half metres deep. It would often have water lying in it. Then there was a stretch of exposed ground protected by

THE DITCH OF THE ANTONINE WALL AT WATLING LODGE 2005 ZZZ05012 (David Elliot)

Falkirk is fortunate in having within the town the most visible segment of the Roman ditch.

concealed pits with spikes at the bottom; and lastly the rampart, over four metres wide and three metres high, with a wooden palisade or fence adding another metre or two.

The wall has been traced from the Forth on the east snaking through Mumrills, Laurieston, Callendar Park, the Pleasance, Arnot Hill, across Maggie Wood's Loan, to Port Downie, Watling Lodge, Rough Castle and so on to the Clyde at Old Kilpatrick. Nearly 2,000 years after it was built, the ditch is still clearly visible in Callendar Park, and at Watling Lodge it is truly impressive. The Roman remains in and around Falkirk are not just of local but of European significance.

Forts were built along the wall. Mumrills,

just east of Laurieston, was one of the largest, and Rough Castle, near Bonnybridge, was one of the smallest. Midway in between, there was a fort at the Pleasance. Watchtowers were built between the forts. Camelon fort sat north of the wall, safeguarding a harbour on the River Carron and the main route north to Perth. The site lies under the Alexander-Dennis and former Wrangler factories on the north side of Glasgow Road, extending under the railway line into Carmuirs golf course. The fort at the Pleasance, like all forts, attracted local people to settle close by, thus creating the first sizable settlement at Falkirk.

In about AD 165 the Romans abandoned the wall for good. We don't know whether the wall was overwhelmed by the Celts or public spending cuts decided in Rome were the cause. The Romans still sent troops north from time to time, but the land that was to become Scotland was no longer under Roman occupation. It was to be nearly 1,800 years before Falkirk once again saw Mediterranean food and wines, running water, sewage systems, central heating and hot baths!

ROUGH CASTLE

At Rough Castle you can follow the line of the Roman road up the steep hill to the fort. The ramparts, the main ditch and the lilia are clearly visible. Lilia were oval pits about one metre long and about a third of a metre deep. Two sharpened and fire-hardened stakes were stuck at the bottom, pointing upwards. The soldiers, with a macabre sense of humour, called them lilies. The pits were covered with vegetation to hide their presence.

LILIA AT ROUGH CASTLE AFTER EXCAVATION
c1905 ZZZ05013 (Falkirk Council Cultural Services)

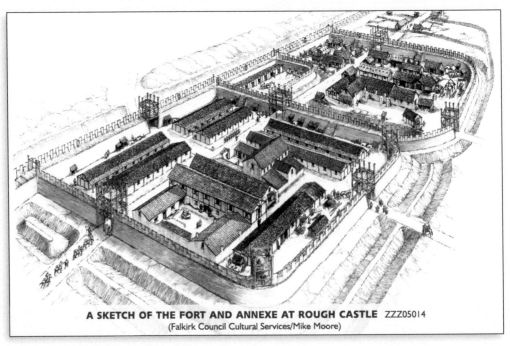

A SKETCH OF THE FORT AND ANNEXE AT ROUGH CASTLE ZZZ05014
(Falkirk Council Cultural Services/Mike Moore)

The wall remained as an everyday presence for locals, farmers and travellers, an obstacle to north-south journeys. The might of imperial Rome, which had built and manned it, was quickly forgotten.

Fact File

Tradition has it that the Antonine wall was called Grim's Dyke because it was breached by a Celtic force led by Grim or Graham, hence Grahamsdyke Street in Laurieston. However, the story is unlikely to be true as the name Graham dates from the Middle Ages.

The Falkirk area was therefore left once more to the Celts. There is little physical evidence to tell us what happened in these aptly named Dark Ages. By the 9th century, several powerful kingdoms met here - the Germanic Anglia of Northumbria, the Welsh-speaking Britons of Strathclyde, and the Picts of Alba. The Scots, who had come from Ireland and who would in due course give their name to the whole country, were spreading out from Argyll.

Despite being on such a frontier, Falkirk was chosen as the site of one of the first churches. From the sacred isle of Iona, St Columba sent out Gaelic-speaking missionaries to spread the Celtic Church. It is thought St Modan established a cell on the hill above the Roman wall, around AD 600, where the Old Parish Church stands today. Christian worship has therefore taken place on the site for about 1,400 years. By the 11th century a church had been built, the so-called 'speckled' church. Why speckled? Perhaps because the stones came from more than one quarry, or from a Roman fort, or from the boulder clay dumped by the glaciers, or because the church was part stone and part wood. It has even been suggested that it was the congregation that was speckled or freckled. But maybe it wasn't speckled at all.

WHAT'S IN A NAME?

The history of the town's name is complicated. It probably started as 'Egglesbreth' in the language of the Britons of Strathclyde, meaning the 'church of Brych'. Brych might have been an early Christian martyr. When Gaels became dominant, they called it 'An Eaglais Bhreac', because that sounded the same as the old name, but it meant something different: the speckled church. (Over 1,000 years later, Gaelic speakers still call Falkirk 'An Eaglais Bhreac'.) In the 12th century it was translated into Latin as 'Varia Capella', into Norman French as 'la Veire Chapelle' and Scots/English as 'Faw Kirk', 'Faw' meaning speckled. In 1458, a scribe was writing in English and was changing Scots words into English, for example, 'wa' to 'wall' or 'ba' to 'ball'. For 'Faw' he wrote 'Fal', wrongly introducing the letter 'l' into Falkirk. Gradually this spelling took over. But those Bairns today who call their town 'Fawkirk' have got it right, and are maintaining a linguistic tradition over 800 years old.

The church served a huge area stretching from Castlecary to Polmont. Scotland, united under Kenneth MacAlpine in AD 844, was now under the feudal system, in which the king and lords gave the use of land in exchange for service. In 1166 the bishop of St Andrews granted the church and land at Falkirk to the Augustinian monks of Holyrood Abbey in Edinburgh. The abbeys were the great powerhouses of the economy. The monks may have built the mill on the East Burn at what is still known as Ladysmill, named after Our Lady. They improved agriculture. But the local folk were just peasants, who had to give free labour to the monks, cutting peat, collecting firewood, helping with the harvest and even soldiering. Any surplus wealth was sent to the abbey at Holyrood. For most folk, life was a struggle for food and against disease, with only dusk bringing relief from toil.

In 1990, a team led by Geoff Bailey, the local archaeologist, carried out an excavation a mile to the east of the church, on a site

THE THANE'S HALL
ZZZ05017 (Falkirk Council Cultural Services/Graeme Sumner)

Fact File

There is a 'foundation stone' high on the wall in the vestibule of the Old Parish Church. It names King Malcolm Canmore as the church's founder in 1057. But the year is written in Arabic numerals at a time when Roman numerals were normal. It is probably a forgery, and Dr James Wilson, the minister in 1800, is suspected of being the culprit.

THE 'FOUNDATION STONE' IN THE OLD KIRK
2005 ZZZ05015 (David Elliot)

THE INTERIOR OF THE THANE'S HALL
ZZZ05016 (Falkirk Council Cultural Services/Graeme Sumner)

now occupied by Callendar Business Park. They discovered the postholes of a wooden building, 25 metres long and seven metres wide, which radio-carbon dating showed to be from the 10th century. It probably belonged to the Thane of Callendar, appointed by the king to enforce his rule. The Thane's Hall was the only substantial building apart from the church. It was a gathering place, a centre for the administration of justice, and where the thane provided hospitality and entertainment for his followers.

The lands of Callendar were certainly worth having. They stretched over a vast distance, from the River Carron in the north to the Avon in the south, apart from Falkirk itself and the lands of Kerse and Dalderse to the northeast. Falkirk did not exist as such. The inhabitants were self-sufficient farmers living in clachans or fermtouns. The land was less productive than now so hunting and fishing for food was still important. Gaelic remained the main language and the people lived in big family groups.

In 1234, King Alexander II decided to reduce the power of the thanes and gave some of the lands of Callendar to Holyrood Abbey. So in addition to the revenues from the huge parish of Falkirk, the canons of Holyrood now owned the land between the Westquarter and Gilston Burns, to become known as Abbots Kerse.

In about 1450, the church was demolished and a new building in the shape of the cross was built. It had a square stone tower resting on four stone piers, with an upper part of timber and slate. Although the church was

A GABLE MARK ON THE OLD PARISH KIRK 2005
ZZZ05018 (David Elliot)

rebuilt in 1811, parts of the 1450 building still remain. You can see the square tower and the old gable marks on the east external wall. Two of the piers that support the tower are visible in the south wall of the vestibule.

A period of relative peace and prosperity in Scotland came to a brutal end in 1296 when Edward I of England invaded. After the rape and pillage of Berwick, Edward advanced through the country taking all before him. A resistance movement led by the great patriot William Wallace had a stunning victory over the English army at the Battle of Stirling Bridge in September 1297. But in June next year, Edward I returned with his biggest army ever, many of whom had recently fought in France. They moved faster than Wallace expected and soon Edward was at Linlithgow.

By 22 July, Wallace had his army drawn up on high ground. Tradition suggests this was at Wallacestone, and certainly such a position gives a commanding view. Whether or not this site squares with the other tradition that the battle was fought in the area of Falkirk's Victoria Park or Mungal, is another story. Low-lying land was usually boggy and would not be a first choice for a battle, although the fighting may have spilled down into these areas. Little physical evidence of the location can be expected, as battlefields were scoured for anything of value after the battle was over. One day we may find the common grave pits of the soldiers who died.

Wallace's army was about 30,000 strong, the same size as the forces they faced. Because Wallace was of more modest birth, many Scottish lords found it hard to take orders from him. And because they owned land in England, they had much to lose. Whereas Edward had the total commitment of his lords, Wallace was not so fortunate. As the

THE WALLACE STONE 2005 F248701k (David Elliot)

ERECTED
to the
MEMORY
of that
CELEBRATED
SCOTTISH HERO
SIR WILLIAM
WALLACE
2nd August
1810

This stands in the village of Wallacestone, in the park at the junction of Wallacestone Brae and Standrigg Road. Erected in 1812, it is one of the earliest memorials to the freedom fighter.

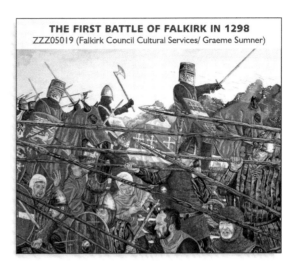

THE FIRST BATTLE OF FALKIRK IN 1298
ZZZ05019 (Falkirk Council Cultural Services/ Graeme Sumner)

lords were professional soldiers, trained since birth, this was to prove crucial.

The Scots troops formed into schiltroms, circular formations of spearmen, making a kind of human hedgehog. Between them were archers, and behind them the cavalry. The ranks of projecting spears made the schiltroms almost impossible for cavalry to penetrate. And so it proved when the first ranks of English cavalry rode up the hill. Horses were impaled on the spears and their riders hauled down and stabbed. A second assault was also repelled. But then the new weapon, the longbow, was deployed with devastating effect. The arrows rained down on the close-packed Scottish troops. Wallace turned to order his cavalry to break up the archers, but they had deserted the field. The English cavalry attacked again, and this time there were gaps in the schiltroms. The defensive lines were breached and the schiltroms destroyed. The battle now spilled out over a wide area and the Scots were routed. Wallace fled to the Torwood.

BRIANSFORD OR BAINSFORD?

An English knight, Brian de Jay, while chasing his enemy over a river crossing, came off his horse when it stuck in the mud. He then fought desperately on foot, but was soon killed. Some say the location was called Briansford, later changing to Bainsford. The more mundane but more credible explanation is that it was named after a stonemason called Bain, who lived there several centuries later.

The Stewarts of Bute put up a tremendous fight, and even when Sir John Stewart was mortally wounded, his men would not desert him. They fought on until all were dead. Nearly 600 years later, the Marquis of Bute erected a Celtic cross at the western entrance to the parish church.

Sir John Stewart himself was buried at the other end of the churchyard under a gravestone that may be the original 13th-century one. It is on the right of the entrance from Manse Place. The inscription, which dates from the 19th century, reads 'Here lies a Scottish hero, Sir John Stewart, who was killed at the Battle of Falkirk 22 July 1298'.

In 1841 Oddfellows Lodge, a charitable society, was dedicated to a major casualty of the battle, Sir John de Graeme, and in the 19th century marches were held in his name. (Oddfellows Hall still stands in Grahams Road.) In 1912 Robert Dollar erected a fountain in his memory in Victoria Park. The plaque on it states that Graeme 'fell near here' but whether that is so is not certain. Sir John's name is perpetuated today by Graeme High School. In 1975, Lewis Lawson, the fondly remembered principal teacher of history at that school, summed up the consequences of the battle:

THE BUTE MEMORIAL 2005 F248702k (David Elliot)

The inscription reads 'In memory of the Men of Bute under Sir John Stewart on 22 July 1298, in the Battle near the Fawe Kirk, fought bravely and fell gloriously, this Cross is reverently raised by John Stuart, Marquess of Bute AD 1877'.

SIR JOHN DE GRAEME

Sir John was a young man who fought with Wallace at Stirling Bridge. Blind Harry in his epic poem tells how he died. De Graeme, seeing Wallace surrounded, engaged and killed an English knight. But a second English knight, spotting a gap in his coat of mail, 'in his bowels thrust his bloody spear'. Graeme, despite this mortal wound, rushed the knight to the ground and killed him, before dying himself. 'Enraged at the loss of Graeme that day, He (Wallace) cut down all that came his way.' Later, Wallace hugged and kissed Graeme's dead body, and promised his death would be avenged. 'No man there from weeping could refrain'.

THE TOMB OF SIR JOHN DE GRAEME 2005
F248703k (Elspeth Reid)

In 1860 a public subscription funded the magnificent wrought iron cupola.

'So the dead pits were dug and mothers and widows mourned, and Edward could boast of victory and take satisfaction in the fact that Wallace was unlikely again to be a powerful force in the land. Yet, hard-headed man of the world that he undoubtedly was, did he really believe that he had finally hammered the Scots? Testimony to the futility of war came only 16 years later when across the very fields where the English had raised their triumphant huzzas, streamed the sorry remnant of another English force fleeing from Bannockburn where Robert Bruce, one of the nobles who treacherously defected from Wallace's command at the crucial moments of the fight at Wallacestone, effectively forged with blood and iron the Scottish nation which Edward had hoped to bury on Saint Magdalene's Day in the charnel pits at Falkirk.'

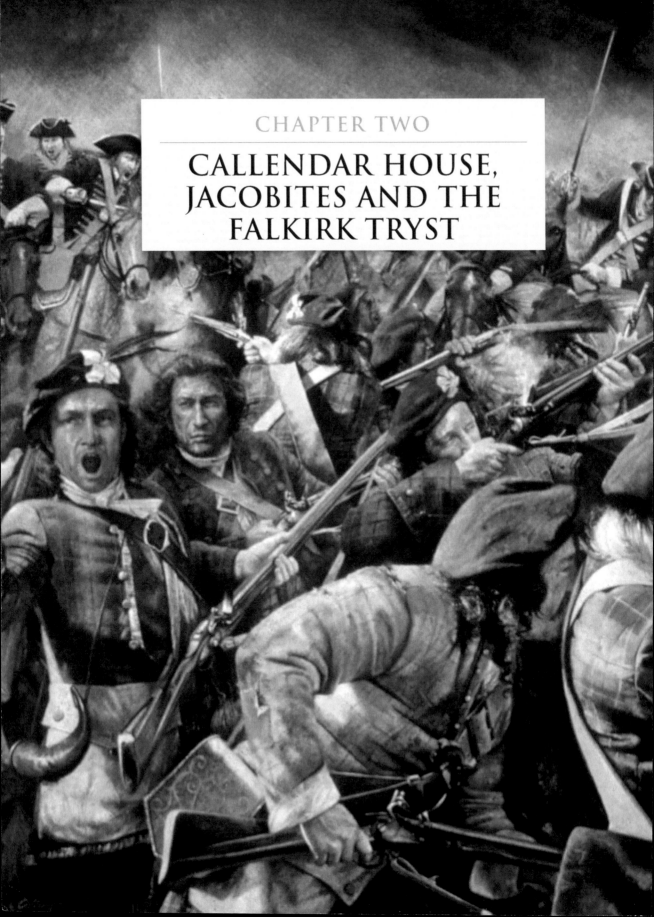

CHAPTER TWO

CALLENDAR HOUSE, JACOBITES AND THE FALKIRK TRYST

THE LIVINGSTONS OF CALLENDAR

The 14th century saw a new family taking up residence at Callendar House. Unwisely, Patrick of Callandar took up arms against King David II and as a punishment lost his estate. In 1346, the king granted the estate to Sir William Livingston. To make certain of his title, Sir William married Christian, daughter of the ousted Patrick.

The Livingstons wanted better than the thane's wooden hall and set about building themselves a stone tower. The original tower, with its massive thick walls, still exists but is hidden within the present day Callendar House. The house, and the Livingston family, were to play a crucial role in the history of Falkirk and of Scotland. The third Livingston, Sir Alexander, raised the young King James II and, until the king was old enough to take over, Sir Alexander ruled the country.

The Livingstons prospered from their rule over the lands of Callendar and were able to extend Callendar House with an east wing. It was now fit to accommodate a queen.

THE LIVINGSTON EFFIGIES 2005 ZZZ05020 (David Elliot)

THE LIVINGSTON EFFIGIES 2005 ZZZ05021 (David Elliot)

The effigies of two leading Livingstons, possibly Alexander and William, and their ladies, lie in the eastern passage of the parish church. Unfortunately the effigies were exposed to the weather during most of the 19th century.

MARY STEWART, QUEEN OF SCOTS

When King James V died he said of the Stewart monarchy 'It cam we a lass and it'll gang wi a lass'. The lass in question was his infant daughter, Mary. From the outset, the Livingston family were utterly loyal to the child who was to become so famous. The Scottish Privy Council made Sir Alexander Livingston one of Mary's guardians, and she spent many of her earliest days at Callendar House. It was here that a meeting of nobles rejected the marriage proposed by King Henry VIII of England between his infant son and the infant Mary. King Henry responded by invading, and Sir Alexander's son, with men from the estate, formed part of the Scottish army which tried to stop him at the Battle of Pinkie in East Lothian. Sadly, the Scottish army was defeated and the son and many of his men were killed. The English pressed on with their 'rough wooing', and it was decided that Mary would be safer in France. Sir Alexander sailed with her, as did his daughter Mary Livingston, one of the Queen's 'Four Maries'. Sir Alexander was to die in France, but his daughter stayed close to the queen for much of her life.

Back in Scotland, the new Lord Livingston, William, was an enthusiastic supporter of the Protestant reformation. The church had become corrupt and was swept away. But William's loyalty to the devout Catholic queen was undiminished. He sailed to France to invite her back to Scotland and after her return in 1561 she was a frequent visitor to Callendar House. As late as 1927 there were rooms in the house decorated with the lion rampant, the thistle and the letter M, and an inscription with dates of her visits. Mary held William in high regard. She came to the christening of a Livingston child, despite a hazardous journey and it being a Protestant service. On another occasion she stayed over on the way back from Glasgow to Edinburgh with her sickly husband, Lord Darnley. Livingston fought with her at Langside, and when she went into exile in England, he and his wife Agnes followed. Their autobiographies would have made fascinating reading.

William was succeeded by his son, another Alexander. King James VI placed his daughter Elizabeth under Alexander's protection, and part of her childhood was spent at Callendar House. Elizabeth married Frederick of Bohemia, which decades later gave the Hanovarians their claim to the throne of the United Kingdom.

In 1600 Falkirk was made a burgh of barony and Alexander Livingston became its Baron Bailie. Following the reformation, the town and the land to the north and east which had

---

Fact File

The famous ballad 'Mary Hamilton' has the verse:

> *'Yestreen the Queen had four Maries*
> *Tonight she'll hae but three*
> *There was Marie Seton and Marie Beaton*
> *And Marie Carmichael and Me'.*

Although not named, Mary Livingston of Callendar was one of the four Maries.

belonged to the abbots of Holyrood, came by a roundabout route to the Livingstons. Thus in 1606 Alexander extended his control over all of Falkirk, bringing it together under one person for the first time. In the same year he was made the first Earl of Linlithgow. The Livingston's loyalty to the royal house of Stewart was strained however when Charles I imposed bishops on the Kirk. Livingston and his Falkirk men went out under General Alexander Leslie and helped defeat the king's army. Politics in those days were just as complicated as now, and before long the earl and his men were in England fighting for the king against Oliver Cromwell's New Model Army. On the losing side, rather than surrender the Falkirk contingent broke

THE TOWN WALL

'It is statute and ordanit that ilk quarter of the toune of Falkirk come forth dey aboute for buildeing of ane dyk about the said burgh for keipeing forthe of streingeris sua that nane mey enter bot at the ports thairof viz. the eist and west portis, kirkwynd, pantaskenes wynd and kow wynde.' Court Book of Falkirk, 1647. The houses on the High Street had long rigs of land running down to the town dyke. There was a port (door) on each of the roads into the town. These were closed at night and burgers took turns at keeping watch. Even by the 1750s the town was small, stretching from the East Port (the Callendar Shopping Centre) to the West Port (just west of the parish church - the Lint Riggs were outside the dyke). The Kirk Wynd Port was about level with modern Bank Street. Bantaskine Wynd Port and Cow Wynd Port were about the same distance to the south.

through the opposing ranks and made their way home. But they had fought without the kirk's approval and had to face a Presbytery enquiry. Livingston fled to Holland to join the Prince of Wales, and the Scottish Parliament banned him from returning.

Despite the kirk's concern about men going down to England to fight for the king, both the kirk and the Scottish Parliament were taken aback when the English, without consultation, executed Charles I. He was, after all, King of Scots too. Scotland therefore accepted the return of his son, Charles II, from Holland. But to Cromwell this was a provocation, and he was not long in invading Scotland. The English army defeated the Scots at Dunbar in 1650. In 1651, Cromwell controlled the area right up to the Scots position at Torwood. But Callendar House was still held by a Scots garrison and was sending out raiding parties to harry the occupying forces. Cromwell decided the house had to be taken and gave the task to the fearsome General Monck with about 300 men. Twice the governor of the garrison, Lieutenant Galbraith was offered terms of surrender and twice he refused. Artillery was brought in and after a short bombardment on 15 July the walls were breached and the house was stormed. The garrison fought to the death. Over 60 men, including Lieutenant Galbraith, were slain; about 16 wounded and 17 male and female civilians were taken prisoner. The dead were buried outside the house and indeed human bones were discovered during landscaping work 150 years later. It does seem somewhat odd that in the 1930s the town council thought it appropriate to name two local streets after Cromwell and Monck and at the same time to ignore Galbraith.

Falkirk now suffered the fate of an occupied town. The English garrison requisitioned sheep, cattle and corn. Tensions rose when some local women fraternised with the soldiers, leading to outbursts of brawling in the street. But peace returned in 1660, when Charles II was restored to the throne and the Earl of Callendar came back to Falkirk.

THE SECOND BATTLE OF FALKIRK

The long rule of the Stewarts had come to an end to be replaced by the Hanoverian line. The 'wee German lairdie' was not universally popular, however, and the Jacobites longed to see the return of the Stewarts. James Livingston was a Jacobite and turned out with his men of Falkirk to fight at Sheriffmuir. In a repeat of history, the Callendar estate was forfeited and James fled into exile. Thus ended, after 370 years, the Livingston's ownership of the lands of Callendar. However James's daughter, Ann, married Lord Kilmarnock, another Jacobite, and they rented the house and lands from the new owners, the York Building Company of London.

The news in August 1745 that Prince Charles Edward Stewart had landed in Moidart and was leading a large Highland army down to Edinburgh aroused fear in Falkirk hearts. Each day the army drew closer, and was soon at Stirling. Their fears seemed justified when the Highland army duly arrived at the West Port on the 15th of September. However, the army passed through quietly, camping just east of Callendar House. Lord Kilmarnock was pleased to have the prince stay with him. Thus another famous name in Scottish history became linked with Callendar House.

The army marched on in triumph to take Edinburgh, where the prince socialised for a time, before marching into England. But early in the New Year he was back and laying siege to Stirling Castle.

In the middle of a cold grey January day, a pursuing government army under General Hawley marched westwards through the High Street and set up camp just outside the town, using the West Burn and Mungal Burn as boundaries. Soon over 1,000 canvas tents stood in rows in the area now bounded by Hope Street to the east and Dollar Park to the west. General Hawley and his officers obtained more comfortable accommodation, where else but in Callendar House.

Hawley rose early on 17 January and rode along the High Street to his army. His plan was for a day of rest before engaging the Jacobites at Plean. Unfortunately for Hawley, Lord George Murray, the experienced commander of the Jacobites, had no intention of allowing the enemy to take the initiative. He had an army of 9,000 men, twice what he had in September for the invasion of England. He could afford to leave a substantial number at Torwood, flying Prince Charlie's flag. The main force skirted round to the west, fording the Carron and Bonny and began the climb up to Falkirk Muir, to the south of the town. The government army 'went to look for dinner, which was not easy to find'. Falkirk had already been occupied for two weeks by the Highland army; food was scarce and prices were high.

One old description of the battle suggests that the countess of Kilmarnock, who was by all accounts a charming hostess, detained Hawley at Callendar House for the whole forenoon, when he needed to be with his army. When eventually he did ride up to his army it was in some haste, and he was a bit dishevelled… but it could be just ancient Jacobite propaganda.

Amazingly, the Highland army managed to circle around undiscovered from Torwood to the muir above the government camp. It was in early afternoon when a gentleman volunteer rode into the government camp crying 'Gentleman, what are you about? The Highlanders will be upon you!' The local folk, caught between the two armies in scenes familiar to us from modern wars, grabbed their children and what goods they could carry and streamed away to safety. On the other hand, some two to three thousand spectators congregated behind government lines to witness the battle.

Hawley tumbled to the enormity of the danger and his men, being trained and disciplined soldiers, mobilised quickly. They had to reach the summit of the muir before the Highlanders, and set off up Maggie Wood's Loan. This was outside the town, and the way was rough and boggy. It wasn't long before most of their cannon were bogged down in the mud. As the troops reached the higher ground, a storm broke and driving rain soaked them through. This being January,

although still afternoon, the light was already fading.

A monument now marks the site of the battle. To the south of it, there is high ground, which falls to what was a marshy area, poorly drained by Glen Burn. The Highlanders won the race to this crucial spot and Lord George Murray positioned his right flank there, protected by the soft ground from the government cavalry. The Highlanders formed a line facing east, with the wind and rain at their back. The government army, many of whom were still struggling to get into

THE MONUMENT TO THE BATTLE OF FALKIRK IN 1746, PHOTOGRAPHED IN 1993 ZZZ05027 (Elspeth Reid)

The monument, erected in 1927, stands at a sharp bend on Greenbank Road, above the ravine.

position, were facing into the gale across the ravine.

Lord George Murray got down from his horse, took off his wig and pulled his hat down hard. Armed with a broadsword and targe he stood in front of the Macdonalds, instructing them not to fire until he gave the order, and so they waited.

The government cavalry attacked first, advancing slowly in the hope that the Highlanders would loose off their single-shot muskets before it was possible to be too accurate. This would then allow a devastating charge into the enemy foot soldiers. But the Highlanders held their fire, and the confidence of the cavalry, already sapped by the surprise march by the Highlanders and the freezing wet conditions, must have evaporated. The cavalry now broke into a gallop to cover the

exposed ground as fast as possible. They could see the Highland muskets aimed directly at them. The Highlanders awaited Murray's order, despite the fearsome sight of cavalry rushing towards them. 30 metres, 20 metres and then when the cavalry were only ten metres away, Murray at last raised his arm. At that range, the muskets were accurate and deadly. Dragoons were blown from their saddles and horses crumpled, but slid forward under their momentum. Those dragoons that made it to the lines were stabbed by Highland dirks. Men and horses screamed and there was blood everywhere. The dragoons turned and ran. Despite warnings not to set off in pursuit of the fleeing enemy, this was too much for the Highlanders to resist. Casting away their muskets, which were too difficult to reload in these conditions, they fell upon

THE SECOND BATTLE OF FALKIRK IN 1746 ZZZ05022 (Falkirk Council Cultural Services/ Chris Collingwood)

the foot soldiers with their broadswords. Government troops fled the field with news of their defeat. But the Highlanders in pursuit now exposed themselves to troops who had stood firm and they were cut down by a volley of muskets. They too fled in confusion, some rushing back to Plean to report a Jacobite defeat. Murray bemoaned that his pipers had taken full part in the fighting, so none could be found to rally his army.

It was a traumatic day for the people of Falkirk. Some had climbed the Steeple to watch and everyone could hear the gunfire. It wasn't long before the escaping dragoons thundered through the town heading for Linlithgow, followed by riderless horses, some horribly wounded, and then the infantry in full flight. General Hawley ordered the burning of the camp and made good his own escape to Linlithgow Palace. He too had a street named after him in the 1930s.

Murray was aware that his men would fare badly if they had to spend the night out on the muir. He announced that 'he would either ly in town or in Paradice'. And so Falkirk was occupied yet again. The troops entered in three columns, Cameron of Lochiel by the West Port, Lord George Drummond by Cow Wynd Port and Lord George Murray by Bantaskine Port. After the few remaining government troops had been dealt with, it was safe to bring Prince Charlie down to the town where he slept the night at the Grand Lodging, which once stood opposite the Steeple.

Hawley spent the night in the safety of Linlithgow. In his first dispatch he blamed defeat on the 'scandalous cowardice' of some of his troops. But he must have slept well because by the following day he was reporting that 'I have given a severe check to the Highlanders' and the retreat to Linlithgow was because of superior accommodation (in the palace) rather than under canvas in the rain, 'otherwise we should have continued in our camp at Falkirk, being masters of the field'.

At daylight the grim task of burying the dead began. Most of the bodies had been stripped naked. An eye-witness said it looked from a distance as if the field was covered in sheep. Burial pits were opened up between Lochgreen Road and Slamannan Road and what is now the wooded area in Dumyat Drive. Others lie buried near Falkirk High Station. Several notables from the government side were buried in the churchyard where their tombs can still be seen. Colonel Robert Munro, his brother Dr Duncan Munro, and a young officer William Edmonstone of Cambuswallace lie there.

A week later the Jacobites left Falkirk, closely followed by the Duke of Cumberland at the head of more government troops. To the relief of the townsfolk, no reprisals were carried out against those who had given hospitality to the Jacobites. However, Lord Kilmarnock of Callendar House was not so fortunate, and in August he was beheaded in London. The Jacobite uprising had already been crushed, in April, on Culloden Muir.

THE FALKIRK TRYST

Each year drovers brought thousands of cattle and sheep down from the Highlands and Islands to Falkirk. Here they were sold

'THE SOLDIERS OF FORTUNE' 2005
ZZZ05023 (David Elliot)

'THE SOLDIERS OF FORTUNE' 2005
ZZZ05024 (David Elliot)

These stained glass windows depict Lord George Murray, Bonnie Prince Charlie and Lord John Drummond. There were made in 1860 for John Wilson's South Bantaskine House. They are now in the Howgate centre.

to cattle buyers from the Lowlands and from England. Falkirk was an ideal location for several reasons. It saved buyers the possibly dangerous journey into the Highlands; it was the natural focus for the drove roads coming down the glens from the north; there was a rapidly growing market for beef and mutton on Clydeside, and to the east there was fertile pasture for fattening beasts. A village of over 60 tents was set up for the tryst, and it was thronged with people. Fires were lit and broth cooked over them. All the Scottish banks, including the Falkirk Bank, were present.

Buyers on big horses roamed through the herds sizing up the beasts and making offers to the Highland drovers on their small ponies. The Gaelic of Uist, Skye, Lochaber, Ross-shire, Angus and Argyll mingled with the Scots and English of the Border counties, Yorkshire and Cumberland. There was much screaming and swearing when one lot of cattle encroached on another's piece of ground. It was one of the biggest cattle sales in Europe and the number of animals sold rose to 150,000 cattle plus thousands of sheep. The tryst was held three times a year, in August, September and October - the October tryst being the largest as it was the last chance for Highland drovers to dispose of their beasts before the onset of winter. It began in the 1700s on the muir southeast of Falkirk before moving to Rough Castle and then, because the Forth and Clyde Canal was now in the way, to Stenhousemuir. There it remained until the advent of the steamship and railways made droving redundant. It brought a lot of wealth to Falkirk.

THE KIRK

After the reformation, the kirk took a close interest in the behaviour of its flock. It was more like the Iranian Ayatollahs than the Church of Scotland of today. No aspect of one's private life was safe from scrutiny by the elders of the kirk. For example, the Kirk Session insisted that all families met in the morning and at night to pray and to sing psalms. Parts of the Bible had to be learned by heart. Fiddle playing at baptisms was frowned on as it led to revelry. Weddings were allowed only on Thursdays, piping was banned because it led to dancing which of course could lead to other things, and the number of guests was limited to 16 on each side. 'Penny weddings' were especially frowned upon.

Funerals fared little better, and funeral feasts and wakes were also banned because they often led to drunken revelry. Sabbath-breaking was another major offence. All working was forbidden, such as 'baking, handling corne, shoeing a horse, picking pease' or 'yoking a pleuch'. Some farmers

---

PENNY WEDDINGS

At penny weddings, each guest brought a small sum of money, or food and drink, towards the cost of the entertainment. In the unlikely event of anything being left over, it was given to the happy couple. The Kirk Session was most concerned about the 'drunkenness and debauche' they caused. Even in the middle of the 18th century, James Scheddings and George Montieth, pipers who had played at such a wedding, were ordered to attend the next meeting of the Session, to answer for their behaviour.

---

must have rued losing a good dry day at harvest time because it fell on the Sabbath. Older Bairns might not find some of this so different from their own youth. But also banned was 'walking fast on the Lord's Day' (unless to the kirk, presumably) and even 'idly gazing from windows'. Elders were sent out to find anyone drinking, either at home or in the alehouse, or gambling. Other crimes were swearing and blasphemy, especially common amongst the fleshers or butchers of the town. More serious were offences of brawling and cheating. The Kirk Session often had to deal with fornication, and any unmarried woman who found herself pregnant was sure to be ordered before it to give up the name of the father. If the couple then got married, the Kirk Session would discharge them from further humiliation.

On Sundays, those found guilty of some transgression were ordered to stand by the kirk door in 'sack claithes' or 'hair goons' for the duration of the service. The sermons lasted about three hours and in winter they must have been in danger of hypothermia. Then they were summoned to take their place at the pillar or the cutty stool in front of the congregation to receive their rebuke from the minister.

The 17th century was a time of dark superstition and any woman who was unusual in any way, muttered a threat or offended some unscrupulous person, could be accused of witchcraft. Banishment, drowning, or burning at the stake after strangulation were common punishments although there is no record of such deaths in Falkirk.

Although life was dominated by a brand of Christianity that was strong on condemnation but weak in compassion, the kirk was trying to maintain public order when there was no police force to do so. It also provided poor relief, funded by a poor box at the church door, endowments and wills. Funds were limited and relief was restricted to beggars possessing a parish token. The token was of pewter and had a drawing of the kirk Steeple embossed on it. An announcement read at the Mercat Cross in the High Street gave beggars from elsewhere 24 hours to leave the town and a week to leave the parish. Any newcomers wishing to settle were questioned closely to ensure that they would not be likely to claim relief in the future. Highlanders were banned absolutely.

THE STORY OF JANET BUCHANAN

In Falkirk in the 1620s, Janet Buchanan accused Christian Watson of witchcraft. Several witnesses testified that Christian was responsible for troubles they had suffered. However, much to their credit many other witnesses came forward on Christian's behalf and 'deponed all in ane voice that they knew nothing in hir but honestie'. The case was dismissed but Janet was now found guilty of making wrongful accusations and was sentenced to stand at the church door for six Sundays at the end of which she was to 'acknowledge hir filthie and abominable fault to the glorie of God and exempill of otheris'. She was subsequently banned from the town and parish, but like a bad penny, kept returning.

By 1632, Falkirk Kirk Session had set up a school, partly funded by the public, as it was obliged to do under Education Acts passed by the Scottish Parliament. It was 'ordainit that all the bairnies within the toune who are past six years of age should cum to the common schule', but most had left by age nine. Attendance was not compulsory so when work on the land was needed it took precedence. Six days a week 'the six hour bell summoned the bairnies to the schule' and it continued until six in the evening, with an hour each for breakfast and dinner. The school was only for boys; girls could be taught weaving and sewing at a private school, but not reading.

THE PLAGUE COMES TO FALKIRK

The plague, or 'peste' as it was called, came to Scotland in 1645. People did not know what caused it or how to cure it and it created great alarm. Falkirk banned travel to infected areas but men returning from the covenanting armies in the Borders brought the plague with them.

The plague lasted for two years. Infected houses were closed up but the occupants were supplied with 'meill and coales'. The victims were buried in a pit on Graham's Muir and in 1647 John Tenant was paid by the Kirk Session for building 'a dyke about the deid'. People avoided the 'pest graves', and the milk of any cattle straying there was thrown away. However, in the early 19th century, the wall was taken down, and eventually the land was built over. The area lies near the junction of Russel Street and George Street.

THE SITE OF THE MERCAT CROSS, IN FRONT OF THE STEEPLE 2005 ZZZ05025 (David Elliot)

Not only was the market held here, but so were punishments such as public floggings, brandings and executions. The last execution was held in 1828.

BARONS, STENTMASTERS AND FEUARS

As a county town, Falkirk today enjoys the same status as Stirling and has overtaken its old neighbour of Linlithgow. But it took a long time.

BARONIAL RULE

In 1600, James VI signed a charter making Falkirk a free burgh of barony. This gave it the power to erect a market cross and to hold a market each Thursday and two fair days a year. The markets were held in the wide area of the High Street at the Steeple. Buying and selling was not allowed in the surrounding countryside; it had to take place in the burgh and the stallholders could be taxed to help run the town.

It also allowed Falkirk to have its own courthouse. The court organised the grazing of the townsfolk's cattle. They had to put them in a common herd to stop them wandering off and grazing on crops of cereals or vegetables.

Guilds (or societies) were formed by merchants, weavers, tailors, hammermen, shoemakers, bakers, wrights, masons, brewers, whipmen and fleshers. The guilds had important rights. For example, on each fair and mercat day, the hammermen could inspect all iron and pewter work being sold by merchants from outwith the town and charge them 'two shilling Scots'. They could also fine those selling poor quality work. Hammermen were craftsmen such as blacksmiths, coppersmiths, and pewter workers, who hammered metal as part of their job.

The town was administered by a Baron Baillie Court. A baillie was an officer of the burgh. Baillie came to mean a lay magistrate, but since 1975 it has been an honorary title only. The court judged on boundary disputes, commercial practices and assaults. It also regulated the town's trade and industry by providing official weights and measures and policing the quality of goods.

Unfortunately, after the Livingston family forfeited the barony in 1715 the court soon fell away. This left the town without any effective administration.

STENTMASTERS

'Were ever people happier than were we
Plentie and Peace bound long unto our shore
From the hot Plague summers Feaver free
When fresh Springs were conveyed unto our Door'

(Michael Livingston of Bantaskine, 1682)

The Falkirk area suffered a severe drought in June and July 1681. At that time, the townspeople had to fetch their water in buckets from the East or West Burns. The burns were nearly dry and people's health was suffering. Alexander Livingston laid a pipeline from a spring in Callendar Wood to the town centre. The pipes were hollowed wooden logs joined together with iron collars. A cistern was built and the water was pumped to the surface through lead pipes to a fountain called the Cross Well. When it opened the following May it gave the townspeople a reliable supply, close to hand.

As we well know today, water has to be paid for. The group of men set up by the earl to look after the water supply was known as the

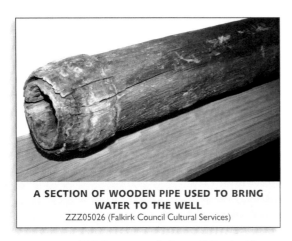

**A SECTION OF WOODEN PIPE USED TO BRING
WATER TO THE WELL**
ZZZ05026 (Falkirk Council Cultural Services)

This is now on display at Callendar House.

stentmasters. Elsewhere in Scotland a stent or tax was usually based on an assessment of property - mainly land - but in Falkirk a sum was decided on the basis of what a person could afford, from a few pennies for a working man up to several pounds for the wealthiest. It was an early form of graduated income tax but, unlike the Inland Revenue, the stentmasters could not force you to pay.

Over the years the well became an obstacle to the crowds and carts making their way along the High Street and so in 1817 it was

PEOPLE AT THE WELL ZZZ05091
(Falkirk Council Cultural Services/Clare Hewitt)

THE LION ON THE WELL 2005 ZZZ05031 (David Elliot)

moved west of the Steeple. The lion that stood atop the old well was reused and is still there today at its new location in the High Street.

After 1788, the stentmasters were still chosen from the guilds but representatives were sent also from each 'o the pairts o the toun' - East Port, West Port, Vicar's Loan and Randygate. They became responsible for cleaning and lighting the streets, maintaining the fire engine and the Steeple, and employing the town drummer to make official announcements.

On display in Callendar House.

THE STENTMASTER'S CHAIR
ZZZ05085 (Falkirk Council Cultural Services)

A NEW OWNER FOR CALLENDAR HOUSE

The Livingston family lost their title to the Callendar estate as a punishment for Lord Livingston's part in the 1715 Jacobite uprising. The London-based York Building Company bought it, but the heirs of the last earl stayed on as tenants, even after Lord Kilmarnock of Callendar was executed for his part in the 1745 uprising. When the York Building Company, which had long been in financial difficulty, put the estate up for sale in 1783, the descendent of the Livingstons who was staying in the house hoped to buy it. Like many housebuyers today, he thought he had offered enough, but was outbid by William Forbes who offered twice the upset price. Forbes was an Aberdonian working

COPPERBOTTOM'S RETREAT

According to one report, 'the inhabitants of the ancient burgh of Falkirk, always noted for their clannish feeling, were in paroxysm' over the Forbes outbidding the descendents of the Livingstons for Callendar House. The Forbes were given a fair bit of abuse when they ventured into the town. One night in 1797 a Forbes, returning from the south through the trees of Callendar Woods, thought he saw the house up in flames, torched by the angry Falkirk mob. He raced to Edinburgh for support and the dragoons were sent out to suppress the fire-raisers. But when they arrived in Falkirk, they found the house intact. What Forbes had seen was the glare from the Carron Iron Works.

in London. He sold the Royal Navy copper sheathing at a good price, to stop worms and weed attacking the wooden hulls. But the Navy attached the copper sheets using iron nails, which corroded and allowed the sheathing to fall off. Forbes bought the copper back cheap. He then showed the Navy how copper nails could be used to attach the sheets and sold them back the copper, again at a good price. For this shrewd bit of business he was nicknamed 'Copperbottom'.

FEUARS

In the 16th and early 17th centuries, the baron feued land in the town to burghers who then paid him feu duties, a tax that older readers may remember paying up until the 1970s. The feuars were given privileges of pasture and the extraction of peats and stones from a muir to the south of the town.

In the late 18th century, William Forbes, the new baron, decided to enclose and improve the common muir. To compensate the feuars for their loss, he gave them some land on the muir. To their credit, the feuars gave part of this wealth to the general good of the town, for example land forming parts of Princes and Blinkbonny Parks. They were also given Callendar Riggs where the fair was held (now a multi-storey car park), and the custom duties from the horse, hay, corn and butter markets.

And so Falkirk muddled along, with the Forbes, the kirk, the stentmasters and the feuars all involved in running the town.

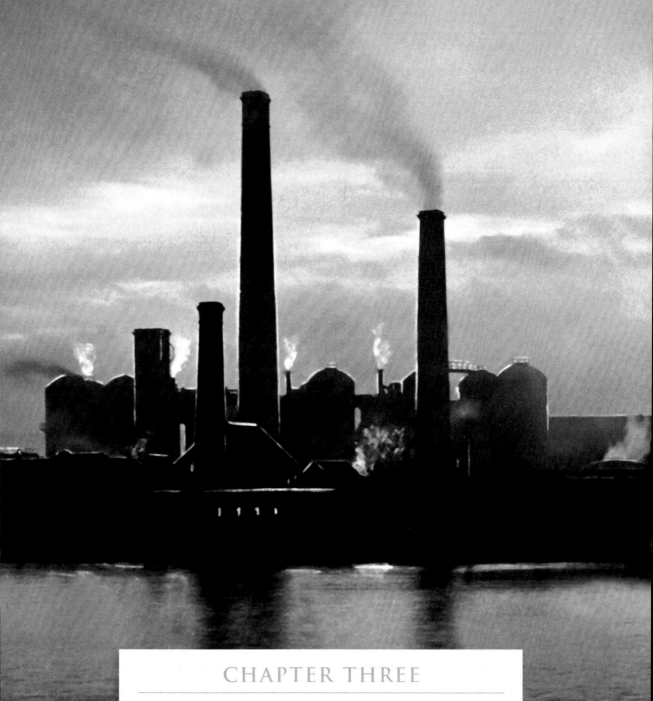

CHAPTER THREE

FALKIRK AND THE INDUSTRIAL REVOLUTION

FOR HUNDREDS OF YEARS Falkirk's way of life had changed only slowly. It was still based on agriculture and the burgh market. But when the red glow of the Carron Iron Works first lit up the night sky on 26 December 1759 it marked the start in Scotland of the well-named Industrial Revolution. It was to change dramatically the way people lived.

Although iron was being produced elsewhere in Scotland, using charcoal made from Highland forests, the Carron Company used different technology and was on a quite different scale. Three men of enterprise set it up. Dr John Roebuck had quit medicine to pursue scientific interests, Samuel Garbett was a businessman and William Cadell was a merchant with coal and transport interests. A site was chosen on the banks of the River Carron at a spot two miles north of Falkirk, where the river provided a good flow of water to drive the cold blast bellows. A short canal to Carronshore allowed raw materials to be imported and finished goods to be exported. There was coal at Bo'ness, Kinnaird, Carronhall and Shieldhill; local ironstone and fireclay, and limestone in Fife. The company planned four blast furnaces, a forge with three hammers, a boring mill, a slit mill and at least four furnaces. It quickly earned the reputation of being the most important foundry in Europe. Its use of Scottish iron ore and coke made from local coal was revolutionary.

Taken from near the site of Forge Row looking southwards towards the Dams and Carron Blast Furnaces.

THE DAMS AND CARRON BLAST FURNACES, CARRON IRON WORKS c1880
ZZZ05028 (Falkirk Council Cultural Services)

Carron Iron Works made a huge impression on people. The minister noted that on a night of low cloud its furnaces lit up the insides of houses, the masts of ships in Bo'ness harbour, Callendar House, Linlithgow Palace and even the steeples of Dunfermline.

The plant was called 'the English foundry' because skilled labour was brought from England, where the industry had been established longer. This caused occasional

RABBIE BURNS VISITS FALKIRK

Robert Burns visited Falkirk in August 1787, spending the night at the Cross Keys Hotel in the High Street. The following morning, the sabbath, he and his friend Willie Nicol visited the tomb of Sir John de Graeme, and then went north over the Great Canal to visit the Carron Iron Works. The porter, however, would not let them in. No visitors were allowed on a Sunday, they didn't have admission tokens and Burns had used a false name. He retired to the Carron Inn, opposite the works, and scored these lines on the window pane:

'We cam na here to view your works
In hopes to be mair wise
But only, lest we gang to Hell,
It may be nae surprise…'

A PLAQUE ON THE WALL OF THE FORMER CROSS KEYS INN 2005 ZZZ05029 (David Elliot)

brawls, for example when a group of English workmen taunted some roadmenders about the uncivilised nature of their country and its inhabitants. The English workers were here to pass on their skills to the locals, but this took longer than expected. Local workers were recruited from agriculture and many came from the Highlands. Their needs were modest as they didn't drink much and a few days' work would pay for 'meal and potatoes'. They would then disappear until their earnings were spent. Few had any experience of industrialised working conditions far less of the specific skills of casting iron or mining coal. As a result, Carron had to overcome a problem with quality. Pots, girdles and axle bushes were simple but steam engine cylinders and guns were not. James Watt worked with the company for a while, building one engine known as 'Beelzebub', but eventually he went to Birmingham to get the precision engineering he needed. The Admiralty took Carron's guns because they were cheap, but after too many displayed a propensity to explode, it cancelled its order and removed all Carron guns from HM ships.

A PART OF THE CAST IRON LINTEL OF THE FIRST BLAST FURNACE AT CARRON 2005
ZZZ05032 (David Elliot)

Both the lintel and cylinder parts are built into the wall of the Carrron Company offices.

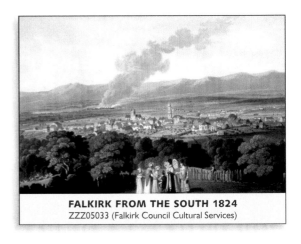

FALKIRK FROM THE SOUTH 1824
ZZZ05033 (Falkirk Council Cultural Services)

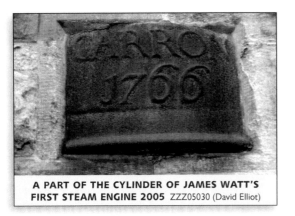

A PART OF THE CYLINDER OF JAMES WATT'S FIRST STEAM ENGINE 2005 ZZZ05030 (David Elliot)

Expertise grew over the years, however. Iron of better quality and a new boring mill were used to produce a completely new type of gun. By 1830, Carron was by far the most successful Scottish plant, with an international reputation based on the quality of its exports. The Carron Shipping Line was established in 1772 to ensure the dependable transport of its goods. Its ships sailed four times a week from Grangemouth and Bo'ness to London until after the Second World War.

THE CARRONADE

By 1778 the Carron Company had redesigned all aspects of the traditional cannon to produce a revolutionary new naval gun. It was short and stubby making it easier to reload but could fire a bigger cannon ball using less gunpowder than the traditional long gun. It was tested at Greenbrae Reach on the banks of the Carron and old cannon balls have been found in the mud near this site. The carronade became popular with merchant ship captains and eventually won acceptance by the Admiralty. It went on to make the fortune of the Carron Company. Carron guns are on display at the former company offices on Old Carron Road, and there are replicas in Callendar House and the Stenhousemuir shopping centre.

A CARRONADE AT THE FORMER CARRON COMPANY OFFICES 2005 ZZZ05034 (David Elliot)

**THE CLOCK TOWER OF THE CARRON COMPANY
OFFICES WITH THE COMPANY CREST 2005**
ZZZ05035 (David Elliot)

FREE HEALTH CARE FOR CANAL WORKERS

In 1789 the canal company generously paid the newly opened Glasgow Royal Infirmary £200 to provide treatment for its workers. The downside was that when a worker was injured on the Falkirk section of the canal in 1790, he had to wait on the next boat passing through to Glasgow to be taken for medical attention. It cost the company nothing to have him treated at the Glasgow Royal, but a Falkirk doctor would have demanded a fee.

The construction and opening of the Great Canal, better known as the Forth and Clyde Canal, also had a big impact on Falkirk. It was built because Glasgow merchants wanted a cheaper way of transporting goods to east coast ports. The Carron Company needed it for its raw materials and finished products. A simple barge canal would have suited them. In Edinburgh the nobility was motivated in part by national pride, a desire to show that Scotland was part of the modern age. They wanted a canal capable of taking ocean-going ships, and so it was to be. It was the largest

construction project Scotland had ever seen and it pioneered organisational and accounting methods which established best practice in both this and other countries for further big projects. Work started under the engineer John Smeaton in 1767, and after a pause at Glasgow the canal reached Bowling on the Clyde in 1790, giving a through-route from Grangemouth. The firm of Clegg & Taylor of Falkirk constructed several of its lengths.

Falkirk was now accessible by sea-going ships from both the east and west coasts. By 1790 the Monkland Canal gave the town cheap access to Lanarkshire coal and in 1822 the Union Canal extended the network to Edinburgh. The two canals were joined at Lock 16, at a large basin called Port Downie. The Union Canal is a 'contour' canal and therefore needed no locks. It hugs the hillside at the same height all the way from South Bantaskine to Edinburgh. It was designed for barges only, not sea-going ships with masts. That is why the Union Canal has stone-arch bridges, whereas the Forth and Clyde Canal had until recently either wooden bascule bridges which opened upwards, or swing bridges.

To connect the end of the Union Canal to Port Downie, a flight of 11 locks had to be constructed. Port Downie quickly became a busy junction and the canal company was persuaded to build the Union Inn to cater for the travellers.

By the 1820s, Falkirk sat at the heart of the Lowland canal network.

A BASCULE BRIDGE ON THE FORTH AND CLYDE CANAL c1900 ZZZ05036 (Falkirk Council Cultural Services)

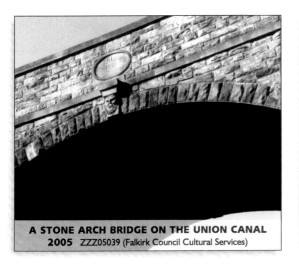

A STONE ARCH BRIDGE ON THE UNION CANAL
2005 ZZZ05039 (Falkirk Council Cultural Services)

TOW-ROPE MARKS ON A UNION CANAL BRIDGE
2005 ZZZ05093 (David Elliot)

UNION INN, PORT DOWNIE 2005 F248704k (David Elliot)

THE CANAL TUNNEL

The longest canal tunnel in Scotland is on the Union Canal. It was built because the Forbes family did not want Callendar House to look onto a canal. The tunnel is 630 metres long. It was cut through solid rock by mainly Irish labour, some of whom were killed by rock falls. A Scot wrote at the time 'few of our countrymen is at it as in general they cannot stand the work'. Years later, a miner, slightly the worse for wear, was making his way through the tunnel one night when a great monster on the towpath reared up in front of him. He ran for his life, convinced the devil was after him. It was, however, only the tow-horse of a barge that had got stuck in the tunnel.

Fact File

One of the bridges, at Glen Village, is known as the 'Laughin Greetin Bridge'. The laughing face looks east and the sad one looks west. One explanation is that the contractor for the west section had a straightforward and profitable task, while the one building the eastern section had the tunnel and locks to contend with.

A FACE ON THE LAUGHIN GREETIN BRIDGE 2005 ZZZ05092 (Falkirk Council Cultural Services)

The canal on the side of the hill was never built.
A tunnel was constructed through the hill instead.

THE CALLENDAR ESTATE WITH THE LINE OF THE UNION CANAL, BY NASMYTH 1817
ZZZ05037 (Falkirk Council Cultural Services)

Boating was a popular hobby.

THE UNION CANAL TUNNEL c1910 ZZZ05038 (Falkirk Council Cultural Services)

THE CALLENDAR ESTATE WITH THE LINE OF THE UNION CANAL, BY NASMYTH 1817
ZZZ05037 (Falkirk Council Cultural Services)

'SWIFT' TRAVEL

Between Edinburgh and Glasgow, canal travel soon replaced bouncing about in horse-drawn coaches. Boats called 'swifts' carried passengers in luxury, with heated cabins, libraries and toilet facilities. The iron boats used after 1830 were towed by two horses at an average speed of nine miles per hour. Falkirk to Glasgow took only three hours and Edinburgh to Glasgow took only six and a half hours. Other boats had to get out of the swifts' way or risk having their towropes cut by the scythe on the swifts' swan-neck prow. The overnight boats were called 'hoolets' because of the sound of their warning horn. The canal boats connected with ships sailing to Ireland, Liverpool, Amsterdam, Hamburg and the Baltic. Passenger numbers rose to almost 200,000 a year.

ALTERATION of HOURS
OF THE
FORTH & CLYDE CANAL
SWIFT
Passenger Boats
To commence 1st October, 1835.

From Port-Dundas.	From Lock No. 16.
At 8 o'Clock, Morning.	At 7 o'Clock, Morning.
" 11 o'Clock, Forenoon.	" 12 o'Clock, Noon.
" 2 o'Clock, Afternoon.	" 3 o'Clock, Afternoon.
" 4¼ o'Clock, Afternoon.	" 6 o'Clock, Evening.

CABIN, 3s.---STEERAGE, 2s.

Passengers for Edinburgh must go by the Boats at 8, 11, or 2 o'clock; for Stirling at 8, 11, or 4¼; for Perth via Crief, &c. at 8; for Kinross, &c. at 11 Forenoon; for Alloa at 4¼ Afternoon; and for Kirkaldy via Dunfermline at 8 o'clock morning.

Fares to these Places Very Moderate.

Canal Office, Port-Dundas, Glasgow, 21st Sept., 1835.   AITKEN & CO. PRINPERS.

A NOTICE ISSUED AT THE CANAL OFFICE 1835
ZZZ05040 (Falkirk Council Cultural Services)

A horse could pull a load of 50 tons on the canal, but only two tons on a good road, so it wasn't long before industry developed along the canal banks - iron foundries in Bainsford, chemical works and tar producers at Port Downie, brick and tile works, and an acid works at Grahamston, a distillery at Rosebank, sawmills at Rosebank and Bainsford, woodyards, corn mills, tanneries, cotton mills and linen mills. The town was transformed. The minister noted in 1785 that there were more surgeons, bakers, clock- and watchmakers and grocers, 'all due to the great canal'.

At this time the population of Falkirk itself was 3,900 with another 600 in Camelon, 800 in Bainsford and 900 in Laurieston. There were on average 270 births a year.

Again thanks to the canal, boat-building was important. Thomas Wilson operated a yard at Tophill with a strong emphasis on research. The site was attractive because it was on a short stretch of canal between two locks. To 'launch' a boat, they drained the canal section, opened the dry-dock gate, then re-flooded the canal to float the boat out. He built the first iron-hulled ship in the world, the 'Vulcan', in Monklands, but he built the second, the

'Cyclops', at Tophill. In May 1835 he carried out speed trials on an experimental steamboat, the 'Vesta'. Archaeologists, excavating the site in spring 2005 before flats were built over it, uncovered the stepped stone sides of the dock, the site of a smiddy, and the base for a steam engine. Port Downie also had a boatyard from 1820 to 1888. As early as 1841 it built a ship of 89 tonnes.

Roads were generally poorly surfaced and to improve their maintenance turnpike trusts were set up. In return for maintaining the road, the trusts were allowed to charge tolls. In the 1790s, two turnpikes were built between Edinburgh and Glasgow, one via Bathgate and the other through Stepps, Camelon Main Street, Falkirk High Street, Callendar Road, Laurieston Mary Street,

THE 'CHARLOTTE DUNDAS'

In 1800 Lord Thomas Dundas asked William Symington of Wanlockhead to design a new steam engine to drive a canal tug. In March 1804 the 'Charlotte Dundas' pulled two barges totalling 130 tonnes for 19 miles towards Glasgow, against a head wind. It was a successful performance and certainly impressed Henry Bell and Robert Fulton of New York. Unfortunately, the canal company stopped further work for fear of damage to the canal banks. Bell went on to exploit Symington's ideas on the Clyde as did Fulton in New York and he is normally credited with the first commercial application of steam power on water. Sadly, the 'Charlotte Dundas' rotted away at Tophill and William Symington died in poverty.

**THE STERN WHEEL ON THE REPLICA OF THE 'CHARLOTTE DUNDAS'
MOORED AT THE FALKIRK WHEEL BASIN 2005** ZZZ05041 (David Elliot)

Polmont and Linlithgow. Although motorways have bypassed it, the road is still heavily used today.

Like industry and transport, agriculture was prospering. The minister in 1795 could report that:

'It is worthy of observation, that in former times of scarcity, the people of Scotland looked up to England, as well as to foreign countries, for supply; but in the present season, when the people of England are in want, we have not only plenty within our borders, but have been able to relieve them in their necessity.'

The land was fertile and well cultivated. Forbes of Callendar House enclosed the land and improved it by adding lime and where it was boggy the land was drained. Crops were grown on a six-year rotation, which included beans and peas. Perhaps that explains the rhyme

'Glasgow for bells
Linlithgow for wells
And Falkirk for peas and beans.'

The canals and turnpikes soon faced the toughest of competition. 1842 saw the opening of the Edinburgh & Glasgow Railway, and the High Station. It was designed, not for goods traffic, but for 'high speed' passenger trains linking the two cities. The carriages ranged from first class, fully enclosed with glass windows and upholstered seats, to standing-room only, in open trucks exposed to the weather and cinders from the engine.

Fact File

The railway company charged the public to have a look inside the High Station tunnel for the three nights before the trains started running. A ticket for the first night was the equivalent of about £15. It is 770 metres long and during construction the remains were found of soldiers killed in the battle of Falkirk in 1746.

In 1850 another railway line was opened, to link the Edinburgh to Glasgow line with Stirling and the north. Unfortunately it created a barrier across the town as bad as the Roman's ditch. It came down over the Skew Bridge on Callendar Road, one of the first bridges to be built at an angle over a road, and continued along an embankment before descending into a cutting. Vicar Street was reduced to a footbridge over the line, wheeled traffic being forced to take a detour round MacFarlane Crescent. Evidence of a blocked off bridge can still be seen there.

GRAHAMSTON BRIDGE, VICAR STREET c1890
ZZZ05042 (Falkirk Council Cultural Services)

As the High Station was up a brae, well outside the town, the new Grahamston station became immediately popular. The third station, on Stirling Road in Camelon, had an island platform. Soon, through company mergers, all three Falkirk stations became part of the North British Railway Company. The railway infrastructure is a testament to the vigour of the Victorian companies and to the quality of construction. Over 150 years later, scores of passenger and heavy coal trains travel these same lines every day.

In the 1970s the Scottish Railway Preservation Society was based in sidings now covered by part of the Central Retail Park, giving its trains easy access to Grahamston station. Along with the well-preserved station buildings it proved an attractive location for filming historical dramas. However, both Grahamston and the High stations were demolished and rebuilt in the 1980s and their goods yards were converted to much-needed car parks. Camelon station had been closed and its access stairs blocked off, but a new station was opened in the 1990s, to the west of the original site.

The railway also served industry, and soon Falkirk was criss-crossed by branch lines serving every factory and mine. There were vast goods yards close to the town centre. The network of tracks was made more complex by competition between the Edinburgh-based NB (North British Railway) and the Glasgow-based Caley (Caledonian Railway). The Carron Company had its own private network with 40 miles of track connecting

At the Falkirk Fair, 'it was black with people'.

STAFF AT GRAHAMSTON STATION 1923 ZZZ05043 (Falkirk Council Cultural Services)

its mines to its foundries. Looking at the Ordnance Survey map from the 1890s, it is easy to understand how the railways employed so many people. It is also impressive how such a complex system was operated safely.

Politicians today are concerned that Scotland does not produce enough entrepreneurs, willing to start up their own businesses. This was not a problem in Falkirk during the 19th century. The Carron Company was a kind of 'university of iron founding', training many men who after a few years left to set up their own companies which would in turn produce workers eager to set up on their own account. Men from the Highlands and from Ireland were attracted by the prospect of employment in Falkirk even if it was dirty, dangerous and hard, and this kept wage costs down. The Falkirk Iron Company was opened in 1819 in Grahamston 'by some gentlemen of the area', employing former Carron Company workers as overseers. By 1911 it was employing 1,130 workers. The Union opened in 1854, Abbots in 1856, Burnbank in 1860, Cockburn's in 1864, Grahamston in 1868, Camelon in 1872 and Callendar in 1876. R & A Main's Gothic Works in Glasgow Road started production in 1900 on a ten-acre site. It was an astonishing time, when Falkirk transformed from a market town to become, if you include the surrounding towns of Larbert, Bonnybridge, Denny and Bo'ness, the home of the greatest concentration in the world of the light castings industry. It was a boomtown, and the population, which had risen to 9,000 by 1851, topped 16,000 by 1901.

The companies made simple goods like grates, drain covers, rones, rone pipes, pots and pans. Then there were heating and cooking appliances of every conceivable variety. Produced well into the 20th century, the kitchen ranges became increasingly sophisticated, with hot water cylinders, roasting and baking ovens, warming ovens, rapid boil plates for the kettle, and cooler plates for simmering. There were designs suitable for cottages, tenements, small houses, large houses and hotels. Others were designed for yachts, cargo ships and passenger liners. Park benches, pillar-boxes, lampposts, railings and, later, phone booths were produced. Another great Victorian innovation was structural ironwork for buildings such as glasshouses, conservatories and railway station canopies. Not only was the domestic market booming, but also Falkirk ironwork was exported to all the corners of the British Empire and beyond.

The process of casting required the design to be drawn, sometimes depicting botanical themes like interwoven fronds and fruit. It was then carved in wood by the pattern-makers, whose working conditions were better than most in the industry. The wooden piece was placed in a moulding box and sand was rammed in around it to take its shape. It was then removed. If the casting was to be hollow, like a kettle, then a core was made to prevent the space filling with iron. The top half of the box was then locked in position and the molten iron poured in. Once the iron cooled, the box was opened and the piece removed. Rough surfaces were ground and polished in the dressing shop.

NEEBOURS

In the foundries, pairs of men called neebours carried a handle each of the ladle containing red-hot molten iron. They brought it from the furnace to pour the iron through a small hole in the moulding box, being very careful not to splash any. The ladles were heavy and forced the men to stoop. It's said that as they went up the road together at the end of a shift, you could tell who held the left handle and who the right, because as they walked, they bent in towards each other.

POURING MOLTEN IRON AT THE CARRON IRON WORKS, c1910
ZZZ05044 (Falkirk Council Cultural Services)

It was hot, dirty and heavy work. Only a few gas mantles were used to light some moulding shops well into the last century. The men wore no protection, other than perhaps moleskin aprons or trousers, even when pouring molten iron. Accidents were frequent. The work was male-dominated, although there were women workers, for example in core-making and in the enamelling shops. This and the heavy manual work in hot conditions meant that a lot of hard-earned wages, desperately needed to support wives and families, were spent in the scores of pubs. Drunkenness was a major problem and it is little wonder that the temperance movement, fighting for abstinence from alcohol, won strong support from the churches and organisations like the Rechabites and the Salvation Army.

Working conditions in the coalmines were in some ways worse than in the iron foundries. Children employed in Carron Company mines reported 'I work on long days 15 to 16 hours'; 'I draw in harness and sister hangs on and pushes behind. The work is gey sair and we often get knocked doon as the cart gaes doon the brae'. In 1842, a law was passed forbidding women and children under the age of ten from being employed underground.

Falkirk became notable also for drink of all types. There were two prominent factories producing aerated water better known as 'ginger' or 'lemonade'. One was Neilson's, long since closed, and the other was Robert Barr's. Originally Barr's factory was at Burnfoot on the south side of the High Street, where in 1830 corks were cut manually for bottling companies. When cork-cutting became

Fact File

The Grahamston Iron Company made a triumphal arch for the Edinburgh International Exhibition of 1886 where it won a Diploma of Honour. It weighs 20 tonnes and is one of the largest cast iron arches ever made. After the exhibition the gates were erected at the entrance to the Grahamston Iron Works in Gowan Avenue, where they stood for 115 years. The Carron Phoenix company refurbished and re-erected the gates in 2002 'as a tribute to the skills and artistry of the ironworkers of Falkirk'.

THE GRAHAMSTON GATE 2005
F248705k (David Elliot)

mechanised, Barr went into aerated water production and eventually took over many rivals. Barr's best-known product was 'Iron Brew', but after the Second World War trade descriptions legislation forced it to re-label its famous drink 'Irn Bru', because it wasn't really made from girders.

Probably of more interest to the men from the foundries was the firm of James Aitken, the brewers. It was founded in 1740 and no doubt the Jacobites celebrated their victory in 1746 with Aitken's beer. In 1797 the firm bought land bordered by Newmarket Street and Hope Street, where it remained throughout its life. Some say Aitken's taught the Australians how to brew good beer, as it was very popular there. The water came from two artesian wells, which supplied 1,000 litres a minute. Continued expansion led to the building of a huge brewery in red brick with a chimney that dominated the townscape. The smell of hops and malted barley pervaded the whole west end.

AITKEN'S BREWERY 1969
ZZZ05045 (Falkirk Council Cultural Services)

The bottle-washing and bottling halls of Aitken's brewery were clouded with steam, and the bottles clanking along the conveyer belts made an enormous noise. The girls wore clogs at work, supplied by the company. The halls were in a basement and you could peer in from windows at pavement level. As a wee girl May Livingston 'used to imagine that this must be what Hell was like'.

Older readers will recall the advert of the tiger whose stripes spelled out Aitken's.

A TRAY ADVERTISING AITKEN'S BEER
ZZZ05046 (Falkirk Council Cultural Services)

For many men, beer was something you used to wash down your whisky, and again Falkirk was well provided. A distillery was opened at Camelon in 1798 and established at Rosebank in 1840, on the banks of the Forth and Clyde Canal. Happily, the canal water was used for cooling purposes only, the water for the whisky being piped in from the River Carron. Unusually it was triple- rather than double-distilled, making this lowland malt very smooth, but most of the output was used for blending.

The 19th century brought higher incomes for many but not necessarily better living conditions, as heavy industry replaced agriculture as the main employer. In the town centre and pockets elsewhere, housing became overcrowded and unsanitary. The town struggled to cope because power was shared between the stentmasters and the feuars. Much against their wishes, the Municipal Reform Act of 1833 stipulated that Falkirk should have a town council with a provost and magistrates. But the Act gave the council few powers. To make matters worse, the only people allowed to vote for it were men of property, most of whom were stentmasters or feuars who didn't want the council to use the limited powers it had been given. The arrival of The Falkirk Herald in 1845 did much to inform public opinion and the pressure for reform grew.

In evidence to a parliamentary committee, the Procurator Fiscal, Mr Gair, declared 'Although Falkirk is my own town, I do not know a dirtier in Scotland'. The piped water supply came from a leaking iron pipe. The source was in the coal wastes to the south. Mr Gair declared the water 'good to drink', although specks of coal contaminated the family washing. Most people still relied on wells, but even these were not free from hazards. A byelaw of 1837 stipulated that 'no person may wash tripe, fish, potatoes, scullions [kitchen cloths] or any other matter at the wells'. In Bainsford and Grahamston, there was no public water supply, so residents

THE FALKIRK HERALD, SCOTLAND'S BIGGEST SELLING LOCAL WEEKLY NEWSPAPER

The Falkirk Herald started in 1845 and was bought the following year by Archibald Johnston, a Falkirk printer. For a while it was published twice weekly and it carried local, national and international news, as it was the only paper people read. It gave a forum through which the town's problems could be highlighted and campaigns mounted. The paper's offices were established on the High Street. In 1908 the proprietor Fred Johnston demolished the original building and opened new offices on the same site the following year. The building still bears the date 1909 and the initials FJ & Co, although it is now occupied by WH Smith. The Herald's office is now located in the Newmarket Centre and the printing works are in Camelon. The Johnston Press now has its head office in Edinburgh and has a turnover of more than £500m. For many years the Herald had a rival, the Falkirk Mail, which was published from 1886 to 1962. The back numbers of both are an invaluable source for local historians.

sunk wells in their gardens and used barrels to catch rainwater from their roofs. In a hot summer, the supplies dried up. Other witnesses described how the only sewer in the town, in the High Street, got choked for want of water to flush it. 'There are very few water closets in the town, and the town therefore presents a most disgusting appearance especially in the by-streets. Away from the causeway road there are nuisances before every door lying there for days together. The filth of Falkirk has become a byeword among all who have known it.' The inevitable result was the spread of disease such as cholera, especially in the ill-drained areas such as Kerse Lane and the Howgate. The mortality rate in Falkirk was 87 per 1,000, compared to 60 in Edinburgh.

Faced with this evidence, it is not surprising that in 1859 the Falkirk Police and Improvement Bill was passed. The

Fact File

In the 1850s there were only a few gas streetlights and some of them were broken. In the winter, they weren't lit on nights a full moon was due, and from April to September they weren't lit at all. The Procurator Fiscal was convinced that the absence of lighting led to street robberies and house-breakings. Even so, one resident thought that street lighting in Grahamston and Bainsford was unnecessary - because the blast furnaces at Carron provided sufficient light. The reality was that the flames created shadows, hiding what was lying in the street.

stentmasters' property, including the Steeple, and their debts, were handed over to the council, and the stentmasters ceased to exist as a corporate body.

THE TOWN HALL, NEWMARKET STREET POST-1900 ZZZ05047 (Falkirk Council Cultural Services/Falkland Herald)

The feuars continued for a time as a separate organisation involved in local government. They demolished their corn exchange in 1878 and built a fine town hall in Newmarket Street. But in 1890, The Falkirk Corporation Act was passed, and the town hall and the feuars' land transferred to the council. Some of their land became Princes Park and Blinkbonny Park. At last, Falkirk had a single local government body, elected by a wider franchise than ever before. The town began to improve.

The population was rising rapidly and the burgh boundaries were extended. In the 1870s a cemetery was created at Camelon and the town centre graveyards were closed. A new water supply was obtained from the Denny Hills in 1891, although it was many years before everyone had water piped into their homes. The West Burn, which ran from Gartcows via Cockburn Street to Tanner's Brae, had become polluted by sewage from the Poor's House and effluent from the tanneries. The solution was not to eliminate the pollution but to pipe the burn underground. Roads were surfaced and cleaned. A fever ward of what became Lochgreen Hospital was built on part of the feuars' land and the people of the town established a hospital in Thornhill Road.

THE CHURCH IN THE 19TH CENTURY

A different kind of improvement was the decline in the Kirk Session's power to invade the private lives of the people. Apart from a small number of Episcopalians, almost everyone in Falkirk was in the Church of Scotland and fell under its tough discipline. But there was a lot of tension in the kirk, primarily over the right to choose the minister. Most Presbyterians felt passionately that only the congregation should have that power. However, in 1712, in breach of the Treaty of Union signed just five years earlier, the Westminster parliament passed the Patronage Act, giving the local laird the right to choose the minister, even against the wishes of the congregation. The Act's effects were dire and long-lasting. It caused many Presbyterians to

break from their church to establish new sects, free to appoint whom they wanted. Ebenezer Erskine led one of the first breakaways and by 1777 the Erskine congregation had built a substantial church in Silver Row, replaced in 1905 by the fine building on the corner of Hodge Street. The 'Anti-Burghers' in turn broke away and built the Tattie Kirk in 1806. The congregation continued to grow and left in 1879 for a new building known as the Graham's Road Church. The Tattie Kirk is now a store for James Syme the ironmongers and can easily be missed behind the buildings in Cow Wynd. However, it is unmistakable because of its octagonal shape.

The octagonal shape was 'to gie no corner for the deil to hide in'. The other tale about the building is that the wooden columns

THE TATTIE KIRK 2005 ZZZ05049 (David Elliot)

supporting the gallery come from a sailing ship taken as a prize and brought home to the River Forth.

In 1799 a Relief Church (that is, relief from the laird's patronage) was built on West Bridge Street. By 1811 the ancient parish church, which had become dilapidated, was demolished, apart from the tower and the pillars which support it. The building that replaced it still stands, one of Falkirk's iconic buildings.

In 1843, at a dramatic meeting in Edinburgh, Dr Thomas Chalmers led 470 members out of the General Assembly of the Church of Scotland to form the Free Church. By doing so these ministers abandoned their church building, their stipend, and their manses. The cause was once again the refusal to accept the laird's right to appoint the minister. 50 years on there must have been some softening of attitudes in Falkirk, however. In 1896 St Andrew's Church was built in Newmarket Street for the Free Church, on land that had been part of the garden of the Old Kirk manse. The Free Church minister at this time

Fact File

Why is the Tattie Kirk so-called?

There are many theories, some less likely than others - it looks like a potato; it was used as a potato store; part of the minister's stipend was paid in potatoes; the congregation was fed potatoes or potato soup after the service; the land next to it was used to grow potatoes.

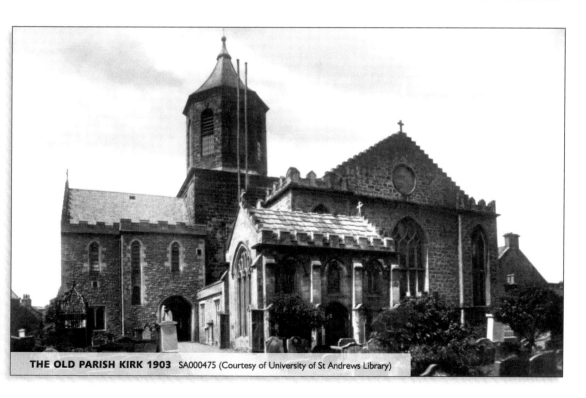

THE OLD PARISH KIRK 1903 SA000475 (Courtesy of University of St Andrews Library)

was Lewis Hay Irving, a powerful advocate for cleaner water and streets, schools for the poor, and better local government. The combination of a rising population and splits in the Presbyterian church caused such a flurry of church building in the 1880s and '90s it is a wonder that stonemasons could be found for anything else.

Large scale migration from Ireland and from the Catholic parts of the Highlands led to the opening of a chapel in 1843 to cater for the growing Roman Catholic congregation. The congregation was more modestly increased by migration from Italy, peaceful arrivals this time who have made a unique contribution to dining out in Falkirk. They were followed during the Second World War by men of the Free Polish Army. The chapel was built in Hope Street, but was destroyed by fire in the 1950s. Saint Francis Xavier Church was opened in 1961 on the same site. It has within it the Polish community's chapel and is decorated by 40 stained glass windows, which are very rare being made from automotive safety glass.

The kirk, enfeebled by dissension, was even less able than in the past to maintain the Scottish system of poor relief. The system had been established to support the deserving poor amongst the parishioners of mainly rural parishes. But Falkirk was now a burgeoning industrial centre with many destitute incomers living in sordid, overcrowded conditions. After 1845, responsibility fell on the burgh, funded out of a tax levied on the better off. But the Scottish principle of poor relief, that for the able-bodied it was to be given only in the most exceptional circumstances, was maintained. Voluntary charitable giving, like the Dorcas Society which gave clothes and boots to the poor, was to be the main provider. No matter what your age, sex or physical condition, if you could not work, the outlook was grim, with the Poor's House in High Station Road the dreaded last refuge.

To be injured at work was also something to dread, as the nearest hospitals were in Edinburgh and Glasgow. Governments didn't believe it was their responsibility to provide hospitals so it was left to charity. Mrs Harriet Gibson, who was married to the owner of the Salton Ironworks, led the campaign for a Falkirk hospital. After a heroic struggle to raise the funds from her wealthy friends, a 12-bed hospital was opened in Thornhill Road in 1889.

EDUCATION

A school of sorts had continued in Falkirk since the first common school in the 1630s. But it was not until 1775 that a purpose-built building was erected, in Back Row (Manor Street). A few years later the minister was able to report 'The grammar school of Falkirk is justly held in great reputation'. In addition to reading, writing and arithmetic, Latin and sometimes Greek were taught to the more able. An additional large room was found in the Pleasance but it too was grossly overcrowded and the teacher, Thomas Downie, complained that the situation was affecting his health; he died five years later at the age of 39. By the 1830s, over 200 children were being educated in two rooms. There

Princes Street was later cut through in front of the school.

FALKIRK GRAMMAR SCHOOL, PARK STREET, POST-1900 ZZZ05048 (Falkirk Council Cultural Services/Falkirk Herald)

were tables for only 54, so they had to take turns sitting at them. Finally, in 1844 the decision was made to build a new school, on a site outside the town. Two years later the new grammar school of Falkirk was opened on the newly built Park Street. The subjects taught in the senior school included English, Latin, Greek, French, German, arithmetic, mathematics, book-keeping, drawing and music. Despite the creation of Princes Street in the 1930s, the building still stands, having served as the grammar school and parochial school until the 1890s, when it became the County Mining Institute. It is now used by Community Education.

In addition to this public school, there were many private schools, in Laurieston, Grahamston, Camelon and Bainsford. These were generally funded from fees and taught a range of subjects, from the basics for young children to bookkeeping for bank clerks. The most celebrated was James Grossart's school in Grahams Road, Grahamston. Opened in 1820, for over 50 years he taught infants in one corner and sailors in another, and almost every subject under the sun. There were maps on the walls, a working model of a steam engine, and a mariner's compass in the centre of the ceiling, surrounded by the constellations, all by his own hand. Grossart conveyed the pleasure of learning through a curriculum combining the arts, science and practical knowledge.

It was a welcome change when the 1872 Education Act took most schools out of the vagaries of fees and charity and funded them from the public purse, open to everyone. (Hence they were called public schools, as they are in the United States.) In 1889 a new building was opened in Rennie Street for Falkirk High School. As a higher-grade school, it could present candidates for the new Higher Grade examinations, which were introduced in 1888. Rennie Street served the school for over 70 years before it moved to Bantaskine. The buildings were later occupied by Woodlands High School before being demolished in the 1990s, to be replaced by flats.

Comely Park School opened in 1879 with a roll of 300, which soon tripled. Only the wall of the old playground with its inscription now survives at the corner of Cow Wynd and Cochrane Street, and a bright new school has replaced the original buildings.

THE COMELY PARK SCHOOL INSCRIPTION WITH THE ORIGINAL DATE STONE OF 1878, PHOTOGRAPHED IN 2005 ZZZ05050 (David Elliot)

Technical education was not overlooked. A school was founded in 1827 to provide courses in science and technology. Eventually it became more focussed on the arts, holding musical evenings in the corn exchange and later the town hall in Newmarket Street. Technical education in iron founding and other industries was provided in the school of arts and sciences, located in a new building in Park Street purpose built in 1878. The building later became part of Falkirk High School, which stood opposite it. However, you can see its original purpose carved in the stonework.

THE STEEPLE

The Steeple is the most prominent building in Falkirk, over 40 metres high and visible for miles around. There probably have been four steeples or tolbooths over the centuries. The first was built sometime in the 16th century. It was replaced about 1660 but there must have been a problem with this second tolbooth because a third was constructed in 1697.

The builder was a Falkirk mason, William Stevenson, and it cost 700 merks Scots. This tolbooth was constructed with its east wall braced against the wall of the courthouse. In 1803 the courthouse was demolished and the tolbooth developed such a lean that it had to be demolished too.

In 1812 the stentmasters set about building what was to be the fourth (and final?) tolbooth. A design by the architect David Hamilton was chosen. Hamilton abandoned the traditional architecture of the Scottish burgh for the clean classical lines which were popular at the time. It was built by Henry Taylor, a local builder, and completed in 1816. The Steeple has four beautifully proportioned stages. The first stage comprised a shop on the ground

floor with a jailer's room above 'for the purpose of confining Strolling Vagrants, and people who commit petty crimes'. The second stage was a fully glazed meeting room. For the third stage, John Russell of Falkirk, one of the best watchmakers of his generation, built a clock with four faces. The faces were lit by gas from 1828. An octagonal belfry formed the fourth stage and the spire was topped by a golden cockerel weathervane. Over the years the stonework suffered weathering necessitating repairs in the late 1960s, but as its bicentenary approaches, it still looks much as is it did when built.

The Steeple in the High Street and the churches were not the only fine buildings which came to dominate the Falkirk streets in the 19th century. As early as 1832, the Commercial Bank of Scotland built the imposing three-storey building with Greek columns in the High Street, opposite Cow Wynd. It was later W Hope's and then Henry Dillon's, ladies and children's outfitters and department store, but is once more a bank. A new sheriff court was built in 1870 and opposite it in 1879 the Royal Bank built the three-storey building with crow-stepped gables and oriel windows at the corner of the High Street and Newmarket Street. Between them stood the elegant cast iron fountain erected by the Gentleman brothers. It wasn't all banks though. Wilson's three-storey building at 105-111 High Street was built by John Wilson of the now demolished South Bantaskine House. You can see the name and date of 1848 just below the roof. In 1886, Mathieson's the bakers built 73 High Street, with its shell apex, crowned by a unicorn bearing a shield, but missing its horn.

**A SKETCH OF THE
18TH-CENTURY TOLBOOTH** ZZZ05051
(Falkirk Council Cultural Services/Clare Hewitt)

Fact File

Steeple struck by lightning

In June 1927, the Steeple was struck by lightning and about ten metres of the spire cascaded to the ground. No-one was injured but one of Barr's horses, yoked to its cart of aerated water, was crushed to death. The spire was quickly rebuilt, and Russell's clock was replaced. The original clock and two of the faces were restored and can be seen, still working, in the National Museum in Edinburgh.

THE STEEPLE DAMAGED BY LIGHTNING 1927
ZZZ05052 (Falkirk Council Cultural Services/Falkirk Herald)

Falkirk's first post office opened in 1689 but in 1893 a new custom-built post office was opened in Vicar Street. In 1922 the telephone exchange was installed there too. The building still stands, bearing its coat-of-arms, but it was replaced by the current building in Garrison Place in 1971. Again the banks led the way in Newmarket Street. The Scots baronial buildings on the corner of Vicar Street and Upper Newmarket Street were built for the National Bank of Scotland in 1862. The Burgh Buildings, (now the registry office) were built in 1879 again with crow-steeped gables and an oriel window. The pyramid roof is crowned with fine ironwork and the Glebe Street frontage carries the old burgh coat of arms and motto, with one difference. It reads 'Better meddle wi than the Bairns o Falkirk'. Apparently, it was considered unlucky to refer to 'the deil' on a building. In the same year the feuars built the town hall, an impressive and much-loved building used for all kinds of social events. (Sadly it was demolished in 1968, leaving a grassy space. Following the demolition, the north wall of the parish church had to be supported by a massive retaining wall to stop it subsiding.) The Christian Institute and St Andrew's Church followed shortly afterwards, creating a fine streetscape.

At the end of the century there was also an explosion of house building. Two- and three-storey tenements replaced the cottages on Grahams Road and Main Street, Bainsford, often built by employers to attract and keep workers. Many have date stones, which give a feel for how and when

THE SHERIFF COURT, POLICE STATION AND GENTLEMAN FOUNTAIN, WEST END 1903
SA000474 (Courtesy of University of St Andrews Library)

MATHIESON'S BUILDING, HIGH STREET 2005
ZZZ05053 (David Elliot)

THE COMMERCIAL BANK BUILDING,
HIGH STREET 2005 ZZZ05056 (David Elliot)

THE PLAQUE ON THE BURGH BUILDINGS, NEWMARKET STREET 2005 ZZZ05054 (David Elliot)

The word 'deil' is missing from the motto.

THE GRAHAMSTON AND BAINSFORD CO-OPERATIVE SOCIETY BUILDING, GRAHAMS ROAD 2005 ZZZ05055 (David Elliot)

PLAQUE ON CO-OPERATIVE BUILDING, UNION STREET, BAINSFORD 2005 ZZZ05058 (David Elliot)

the town grew. Some of these buildings can still be seen although the harmony of the long stretches of stone facades has been lost. Excellent housing for foremen

NEWMARKET STREET, THE VIEW LOOKING EAST c1895
ZZZ05057 (Falkirk Council Cultural Services/Falkirk Herald)

and managers was built behind the main streets, such as in Alma Street and Russel Street, and most of it survives today. The co-operative societies were very active and built many fine shops, embellished with the co-op's name and symbols. Some of these buildings also survive.

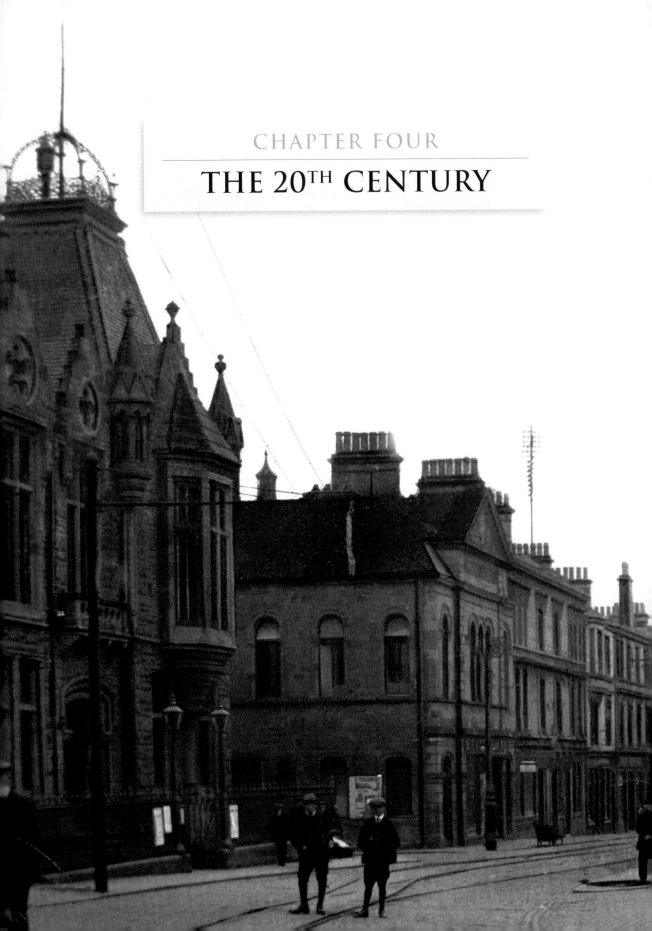

CHAPTER FOUR

THE 20TH CENTURY

NEWMARKET STREET AND THE SOUTH AFRICAN WAR MEMORIAL
c1910 ZZZ05059 (Falkirk Council Cultural Services)

THERE WAS AN AIR of confidence about Edwardian Falkirk at the dawn of the new century. The town now had a unified council to look after its affairs. The rich were getting richer, and a middle class was emerging, which had money to spend over and above the basic necessities. A talented local photographer, Thomas Easton, captured this in portraits of his family. Even the working class was becoming slightly better off. On the wider scene, the British Empire was at its height and the South African War, in which the Boers had humiliated the Empire forces on occasion, was now concluded. The boys had come home and a memorial to their efforts was unveiled in Newmarket Street in 1906, where it still stands today. The monument to the Duke of Wellington and his horse

THREE YOUNG WOMEN, RELATIONS OF THE PHOTOGRAPHER THOMAS EASTON, ENJOY AN INFORMAL TEA PARTY IN THE GARDEN
ZZZ05060 (Falkirk Council Cultural Services)

Copenhagen, which had been erected next to the Steeple in 1854, was re-located to the other end of Newmarket Street in 1905.

Electricity was still a novelty at this time with only a few businesses generating their

KIRK WYND AND MANOR STREET BEFORE STREET WIDENING 1902
ZZZ05061 (Falkirk Council Cultural Services/Falkirk Herald)

Note the new electric lighting. The ornate streetlights with the two lights at a lower level and the main light at the end of the curved pylon were installed in Falkirk's main thoroughfares in association with the opening of Falkirk power station in 1903. Through the night, the smaller lights were switched on and the main light was switched off.

own power. There was no public supply until in 1901 the town council set about building its own power station in High Station Road. In preparation, elegant new electric streetlights were located next to the old gaslights on all the principal thoroughfares of the town, although it was some time before the power started to flow and they could be switched on.

Increasing traffic forced the council to do something about the narrow wynds which ran off the High Street. Cow Wynd, the main route south, was only four metres wide. Fortunately the coal traffic to the Carron Iron Works now went by rail rather than along it and the High Street. It was widened to six metres. Lint Riggs was only the width of a cart and Kirk Wynd was if anything narrower. At the bottom of Lint Riggs was a rag store, which was home to a large colony of rats. Back Row was as narrow and the houses, some of which dated from the 17th century, had become overcrowded slums, breeding grounds for disease. The solution was demolition and new building lines were set to provide streets able to accommodate vehicles and pedestrians. Buildings such as the Royal Bank and Burton's (previously the Commercial Bank and Railway Hotel) on Kirk

CALLENDAR HOUSE 1903 SA000477 (Courtesy of University of St Andrews Library)

Wynd and the public house on the corner of Newmarket Street and Lint Riggs date from this time of reconstruction. The town centre became quite elegant in appearance, reflecting the town's prosperity.

The light castings industry continued to flourish. Other industries such as mining and chemicals also prospered as did the three drinks industries - beer, whisky and aerated water. Hundreds were employed on the railways, the canals and roads. New opportunities for Falkirk workers were created down the road at Grangemouth, where the Caledonian Railway Company was expanding the port, the Scottish Cooperative Wholesale Society had opened a huge soap factory and West Lothian shale oil was being processed at a new refinery.

Shorter working weeks, especially Saturday afternoons free of toil, led to an upsurge in recreation of all kinds. These offered a much-needed distraction from the other great recreation of drinking. Curling had been played for centuries and it was a similar story for golf, although it was not until 1922 that Falkirk Golf Club opened at Carmuirs. The higher part of the land was the site of the

Fact File

In keeping with its drive to rebuild and modernise the town, the council decided to give Back Row a new, posher, name - Manor Street. That one has stuck, unlike the renaming of Cow Wynd as High Station Road. The Bairns resolutely refused to use the new name and eventually the council had to concede defeat.

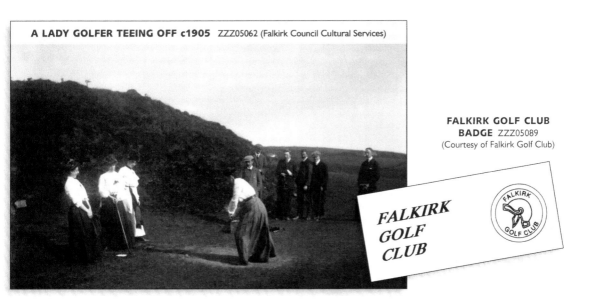

A LADY GOLFER TEEING OFF c1905 ZZZ05062 (Falkirk Council Cultural Services)

FALKIRK GOLF CLUB
BADGE ZZZ05089
(Courtesy of Falkirk Golf Club)

FALKIRK GOLF CLUB

Roman fort, a fact recognised in the club's badge; the lower part was under the River Carron until 1757 and had previously been known as Meg Allan's Bog.

Lawn tennis was a new sport for the better off. Cricket was also popular, possibly introduced to Falkirk in the 18th century by English migrants at the Carron Iron Works. Bowling appealed to all sections of the community and clubs were established in each district of the town towards the end of the 19th century. For example, Camelon Bowling Club was established below the canal embankment at Lock 12 in 1872. Surprisingly, in the 1920s it had a woman president, Miss M L Webster, at a time when full membership was generally reserved for men.

But the great love of working class men throughout the 20th century was the fitba. It allowed a chance to be part of something bigger, unconnected to the disciplines of

EDWARDIAN TENNIS PLAYERS c1905
ZZZ05063 (Falkirk Council Cultural Services)

work, church or even home, and to let off steam at life's injustices as well as your team's performance. Falkirk Football and Athletic Club was founded in 1876 and played its first game against Bonnybridge Grasshoppers. It took place at Brockville, on a sloping site surrounded by hedges. It soon flitted to Randyford, then Blinkbonny, and then to Hope Street before returning to Brockville in about 1885. Despite proposals to relocate being discussed from the 1930s onwards it was to stay there until May 2003. In season 1902-03 the club was admitted to Division Two of the Scottish League and in 1913 the Bairns won the Scottish Cup for the first time. It won it again in 1957. East Stirlingshire was founded in 1880 and moved from Merchiston Park to Firs Park in 1921, where The Shire remains today although perhaps not for long. For a time the two teams competed on an equal basis but Falkirk FC eventually became the more successful.

Another all-male pursuit was quoiting. The game should not be confused with the quoits played on the decks of cruise ships as these were bun-shaped cast-iron rings weighing about three-quarters of a kilo (Falkirk Museums has examples). They were thrown at iron pins driven into beds of

FALKIRK FOOTBALL CLUB BADGE
ZZZ05064 (Courtesy of Falkirk Football and Athletic Club)

clay, known as kiting greens. It was popular throughout the district amongst miners and iron founders.

There were other less competitive sports. The Union Canal, having lost much of its commercial traffic by this time, was popular

AN EARLY GAME AT BROCKVILLE ZZZ05065 (Falkirk Council Cultural Services)

BOATING ON THE UNION CANAL 1906 SA000472
(Courtesy of University of St Andrews Library)

from the bustle and hooped skirt of the Victorians to more practical skirts, worn with the latest fashion of the 'leg-of-mutton' sleeved blouse. It allowed respectable women to travel independently, and for unmarried men and women to mix socially on their bicycle outings. 40 separate cycling clubs formed in the Falkirk area, mostly between 1890 and 1910. Bicycles were built to order by cycle shops, for example Malley, Wilson & Co of Graham's Road produced the 'Brockville'. They also advertised 'all lady cyclists taught free of charge'.

for fishing, boating and walks along the towpath.

One of the great innovations of the late 19th century was the modern bicycle, which quickly replaced the penny-farthing. The bicycle forced women's fashions to change

The railways had allowed cheap travel for the first time and many churches, schools and works organised excursions by train, often including a sail on a steamer on Lochs Lomond, Tay or Katrine or on the Firth of Clyde.

FALKIRK IRON COMPANY WORKERS ON AN EXCURSION ON LOCH LOMOND c1910
ZZZ05066 (Falkirk Council Cultural Services)

BOATING ON THE UNION CANAL 1906 SA000472
(Courtesy of University of St Andrews Library)

The brave might even venture out on one of Walter Alexander's or Scottish General's charabancs. Walter Alexander was a Camelon cycle shop owner. In 1914 he ran a Belhaven charabanc between Bonnybridge and Falkirk, weekends only. The vehicle, made in Wishaw, came with one chassis but two bodies that could be swapped around, so it was a lorry through the week. Bus travel was boosted at the end of the war because of army surplus vehicles and trained drivers. But even in 1930 only one in ten families owned a car and they weren't used for getting to work.

FALKIRK'S TRAMS

Falkirk's tramway was built in 1905 and trams ran both ways around a circular route from Newmarket Street down Grahams Road to Bainsford, Stenhousemuir, Larbert and Camelon. Notorious for the screeching sound of the wheels as they took tight corners, the trams were known as the 'Secret Service'. An extension ran along the High Street to Laurieston from 1909 to 1924. The original trams were built near Paris and shipped in through Grangemouth. They sat 22 passengers on varnished pitch pine seats inside and 'garden' seats upstairs. The interior woodwork was of polished walnut with oak doors and a maple roof. The livery was Prussian blue lined out in gold leaf. There was a tram every 15 minutes, every seven minutes at peak times. Four trams waited for the workers at the end of each shift at Carron Iron Works. In its first year, the system carried over three and a half million passengers.

A TRAMCAR IN THE HIGH STREET, ON THE LAURIESTON EXTENSION ROUTE c1910
ZZZ05067 (Falkirk Council Cultural Services/Falkirk Herald)

A TRAMCAR IN GRAHAMS ROAD c1910
SA000476 (Courtesy of University of St Andrews Library)

Another development which confirmed the feeling of Edwardian progress was the opening of the Falkirk Tramway. Construction started in January 1905 with new swing bridges at Bainsford and Camelon, to replace the old wooden bascule bridges with their curved deck. The stone arch bridge over the Carron at the Carron works was also replaced - eventually; the first explosive charges simply lifted it up and dumped it back in position. Parson-Peebles had the contract and the track and overhead gantries were ready for use by September 1905.

FALKIRK AT WAR 1914-19

Despite the optimism of the Edwardian era, there were constant fears over the threat to the British Empire from the growing power of Imperial Germany. Nonetheless it was still a surprise when war broke out in August 1914. Few realised how long and hard the war would be; yet it was the very capacity of industries such as Falkirk's that allowed the war to proceed on such a vast scale. It was a boom time for the foundries. In 1915, the UK Government took power over munitions production, and foundries became 'Government Controlled Establishments'. At Carron Company, plants were built for the manufacture of shells, aerial bombs, mortar bombs and grenades. Falkirk Iron Company produced much of its munitions, some 10,000 tonnes, at its Castlelaurie foundry. The Germans were first to deploy poison gas, but both sides subsequently used chemical warfare and so Falkirk Iron Company produced gas bombs, the quality of which had to be especially high to avoid leakage while being transported. The company also produced about 22,000 'toffee apple' mortars, some of which can be seen in museums in northern France today. Women, girls and unskilled workers replaced those who had gone off to fight. The women were called munitionettes and their work could be dangerous, though less so in the foundries than in the Nobel Explosives Works at Redding. Some were killed in explosions or suffered health problems such as TNT poisoning from the chemicals they were using. Their skin could become yellow hence their nickname 'canaries'. On average their pay was less than half that of men.

Fact File
Safety on Falkirk's tramway

Where the tramlines went under a bridge, as at the Skew Bridge in Laurieston or on Stirling Road, Camelon, the overhead cable was carried low and to one side of the arch, within reach of someone on the upper deck. However, the company did place signboards on the bridges warning passengers not to touch the live wires. Safety was better at the swing bridges. When they opened to allow boats to pass, the electrical current to the trams was automatically cut off on the approaches to the bridge, there were derailing points for any runaway tram, a gate was closed across the road, and a traffic signal was turned to danger. There is no record of a tram falling into the canal.

**A TRAMCAR IN THE HIGH STREET, ON THE
LAURIESTON EXTENSION ROUTE c1910**
ZZZ05067 (Falkirk Council Cultural Services/Falkirk Herald)

A MOULDING SHOP, FALKIRK IRON COMPANY 1917
ZZZ05068 (Falkirk Council Cultural Services)

MUNITIONETTES FINISHING OFF HAND GRENADES, FALKIRK IRON COMPANY 1917
ZZZ05069 (Falkirk Council Cultural Services)

Falkirk's regiment was the Argyll and Sutherland Highlanders, 7th Battalion, C Company. The crest of the Fourth Volunteer Battalion of the A&S can still be seen on the drill hall built in 1859. It is now the Falkirk School of Gymnastics.

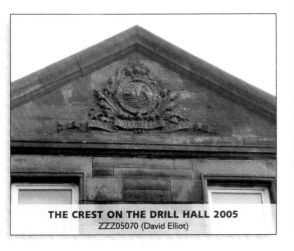

THE CREST ON THE DRILL HALL 2005
ZZZ05070 (David Elliot)

widows and children of those killed that 'they shall be remembered' and they are, each November, at Dollar Park.

THE CENOTAPH 2005 F248706k (David Elliot)

A strange euphoria spread through the town on the outbreak of war and the recruitment office on West Bridge Street was besieged by young men anxious to join up. During the First World War the regiment expanded enormously, to 26 battalions. After it was all over, a cenotaph was raised in Dollar Park. A plaque on it records that 'Over eleven hundred Falkirk Bairns died for their King and Country and in the Cause of Freedom 1914-1919'. This was about one in 15 of the male population and obviously a much higher proportion of the young men of Falkirk. A new meaning was given to the motto on the crest above the plaque: the Great War undoubtedly touched 'ane and a'. The promise was given then to the mothers,

With the return of peace, the demobbed men replaced the women who had taken over during the war and the foundries suffered a slump in orders. However, a national house-building programme funded by the government brought increased demand for kitchen ranges, gutters and rone pipes so that by the mid 1920s there was close on full employment in the industry. By the 1930s the Depression and a slump in the rate of house building caused short-time working and closures. The companies reacted by merging, for example to create Allied Iron Founders. This allowed specialisation, which helped it to survive for several more decades.

The slum clearance programme had

FIRST AID IN THE CASTINGS INDUSTRY

George Aird's father worked for the Forth and Clyde Iron Works. He was paid an extra seven shillings and sixpence a week to provide medical attention to the workers. If a man got a particle of iron in his eye he came up to the Aird's house in Laurieston after work to have it removed. Mr Aird senior used a sharpened crochet needle, which had been rubbed over a magnet to magnetise it. With this he removed the particle from the worker's eye. If the eye membrane had already grown over the metal, then he sent them along to the infirmary.

WESTQUARTER GLEN c1905 SA000473 (Courtesy of University of St Andrews Library)

Westquarter House was demolished in the 1930s and housing built, mainly for former coal miners and their families.

an impact on Falkirk's housing as well as its industry. New houses were built at Westquarter Model Village where miners' families were relocated, and in the town itself, for example on Arnot Street. The largest schemes were at Carmuirs and Bog Road. Several road schemes were implemented. The High Street was widened at the east end requiring the demolition of part of the notorious Silver Row.

VICAR STREET, THE SALON CINEMA AND TUDOR HOUSE RESTAURANT 1939 SA000467 (Courtesy of University of St Andrews Library)

A small hill was removed to create Callendar Riggs. Princes Street was punched through from Park Street to Vicar Street, to connect with Newmarket Street. At the west end of the High Street, Cockburn Street was opened up so that Cow Wynd was no longer the only route to the south of the town.

Robert Dollar was a Falkirk Bairn who made his money in harvesting timber in the west coast of the United States and exporting it to the Far East. He bequeathed Arnotdale estate to the town and in 1921 Dollar Park opened there. The park is less used nowadays as leisure interests change, but there is a proposal to create a garden to celebrate the achievements of another Bairn, George Forrest. Between 1904 and 1937 Forrest brought back more

THE NEWLY OPENED PRINCES STREET AND ART DECO CINEMA 1936 SA000466 (Courtesy of University of St Andrews Library)

than 31,000 plant specimens from China. Robert Dollar also donated a carillon of bells to the parish church, which still rings out over the High Street. They are operated by a set of levers on the floor below the bells.

ONE OF THE BELLS OF THE OLD KIRK 2005
ZZZ05071 (David Elliot)

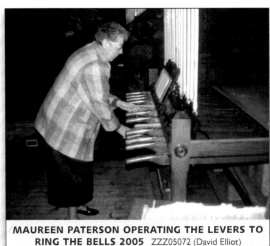

MAUREEN PATERSON OPERATING THE LEVERS TO RING THE BELLS 2005 ZZZ05072 (David Elliot)

Fact File

The Shortest Street

Falkirk has the shortest street in Britain. It is Tolbooth Street, behind the Steeple.

TOLBOOTH STREET 2005 F248707k (David Elliot)

One of the greatest achievements of Falkirk at this time was raising the money for a new infirmary. By the 1920s, the existing hospital in Thornhill Road could no longer cope. A site was soon purchased at Gartcows for a new infirmary. The architect was W J Gibson, son of Harriet Gibson, founder of Thornhill. For five years collection boxes were everywhere: in homes, shops, workplaces, and sports grounds. There was hardly a public event which did not result in more money being added to the hospital fund. Fund-raising concerts, dances, and football matches all played their part. A booklet urged collectors to strap a box onto the back of your dog, and to take your collecting box with you on long train journeys. The final event, a grand

THE OPENING OF FALKIRK & DISTRICT ROYAL INFIRMARY 1932 ZZZ05073 (Falkirk Council Cultural Services/Falkirk Herald)

bazaar held over four days in the drill hall, raised the stunning total of over £400,000 in today's money. The old motto, touch ane, touch a, sums up perfectly how the Bairns rose to the challenge. Building started in 1926 and the new Falkirk & District Royal Infirmary opened in 1931, with 85 beds and 45 nursing staff. By that time the people of Falkirk had raised the entire cost. In the heart of the original building, wooden panels list the donations received over many years, for example from cycle clubs, the Infirmary (Football) Cup, the foundries, and Falkirk Operatic Society. There is a bust of Harriet Gibson commemorating all her hard work.

All these new roads gave an opportunity for new building and Falkirk acquired some fine buildings in the art deco style of the 1930s. The bus station façade has gone but the style of the time can be seen in the

SILVER ROW

Silver Row was an old lane which ran north from the High Street, where the Callendar shopping centre now stands. It had its share of slums, especially at the end nearest the High Street. But it also had fine buildings like St Francis Catholic School built in 1880 and the Erskine Church built in 1777. After the Erskine congregation moved in 1905 it became the Electric Theatre and later the Roxy. It was here that Max Bygraves gave his first public singing performance while stationed in the area during the Second World War. Syncopating Sandy, an old music hall pro, broke the world record for continuous piano playing at the Roxy. Half of Falkirk filed past to witness his effort. A painter and decorator used the basement of the theatre as a paint shop and store. The Roxy was a fire disaster that thankfully never happened.

shops on Callendar Riggs, the corner block at West Bridge Street and Cockburn Street (by the same architect), the former co-op, now Clydesdale Bank buildings, in Kirk Wynd, and the now-closed cinema on Princes Street. It had started life as the Grand Theatre, and was then rebuilt to reflect the ocean liners of the time and renamed the Regal. Castings House, built for the Allied Iron Founders in Grahams Road, is of similar style. In complete contrast and a bit out of place is the Tudor House, built about the same time. A visit to Mathieson's restaurant there, then next door to the pictures at the Regal was a pleasure enjoyed by many.

By this time, Falkirk was well into the Hollywood dream factory with a total of seven cinemas. The Regal/Cannon now stands empty. Another, the Picture House in Bank Street, was previously a church and is now the Carron Works pub. A third, the Salon, was in the building on the corner of Newmarket Street and Vicar Street. Falkirk folk were never content just to watch others perform, however. The town developed a strong tradition of dramatic and operatic clubs such as the Falkirk Operatic Society and the Bohemians. Another great pastime was dancing, the most famous venues being Doak's Palais de Dance, Turpie's, or Mathieson's in the High Street. Another source of entertainment was the ice rink on Grangemouth Road, in which dances could also be held. The building still stands, next to the college, but sadly Falkirk no longer has its own rink.

THE ART DECO BUS STATION, CALLENDAR ROAD 1939
SA000468 (Courtesy of University of St Andrews Library)

THE ICE RINK, GRANGEMOUTH ROAD 1939
SA000470 (Courtesy of University of St Andrews Library)

An unwelcome development took place in 1935. The double deck trams had been allowed to deteriorate and passengers had drifted away to the buses. However, in the 1920s Fife Tramways bought the company and invested in new track and new 'Pullman' single deck tramcars capable of 35 mph. So comfortable were they that people waiting at tram stops would let an old double-decker pass just to enjoy the comfort of the new enclosed ones. There was a car every four minutes at the weekends. Passenger numbers increased, reaching 3.8m in 1934 and the company became profitable. However, in 1935 it was bought by SMT, a bus company, and they didn't want anything to compete with their buses. To the dismay of its customers

the service was stopped on 21 July 1936, the last tram carrying a floral wreath over its headlight. The overhead wires were quickly removed and the track dug up. About the same time, the locks connecting the Union and Forth and Clyde Canals at Port Downie were closed to traffic.

A SINGLE DECK TRAM c1930
ZZZ05076 (Falkirk Council Cultural Services/Falkirk Herald)

THE REDDING PIT DISASTER

One of the worst mining accidents in Scotland took place at the number 23 pit at Redding on 25 September 1923. Water flooded in from old mine workings, killing 37 miners. Local miners, the mines rescue team and divers from the Rosyth naval base were all involved in the desperate attempt to save lives. Nine days after the disaster, five men were brought to safety. They had passed the time talking over their experiences in the First World War. The survivors became local celebrities, and were pointed out in the street to visitors.

THE MEMORIAL TO THE REDDING PIT DISASTER OF 1923 PHOTOGRAPHED IN 2005 ZZZ05075 (David Elliot)

CROWDS WAITING FOR NEWS AT REDDING 1923 ZZZ05074 (Falkirk Council Cultural Services/Falkirk Herald)

LOCK 16, PORT DOWNIE, FORTH AND CLYDE CANAL 1939 SA000471 (Courtesy of University of St Andrews Library)

The bus industry in Falkirk was long dominated by the firm of Walter Alexander. Not only did it provide most of the local services with its Midland line but also long distance services and excursions on its Bluebird coaches. Apart from operating bus services, the firm also built buses in their factory in Camelon. Buses in the liveries of companies from all over the country and overseas, were and are a colourful sight outside the factory.

The population of the town continued to rise, to 33,000 by 1920 and with domestic and industrial water consumption rising even faster, the old problem of a lack of fresh water arose again. The solution was ambitious - a dam was built high in the Campsie Fells which flooded the Carron Valley.

MAIN STREET, CAMELON, AFTER THE LIFTING OF THE TRAMLINES 1939
SA000469 (Courtesy of University of St Andrews Library)

CARNERA, THE 'WORLD'S LARGEST HORSE' ZZZ05077 (Falkirk Council Cultural Services)

Carnera was a Clydesdale owned by Robert Barr. He stood 19 hands (1.98 metres) high. He was so tall he was not well suited to pulling the heavy carts of aerated water, but was used to advertise Barr's Iron Brew. The whole town was saddened when he fell in Cow Wynd and had to be put down.

The Second World War began in September 1939, only 20 years after the Great War ended. The atmosphere was very different, as no-one was under any illusions as to what to expect. Gas masks were carried, the streetlights were switched off and lighted windows had to be blacked out. Not surprisingly people were hurt bumping into walls or each other. Car headlights were cut to slits and road accidents caused many injuries to drivers and pedestrians. Anderson shelters were built for council house tenants and public shelters were built in the Newmarket Street Gardens. Temporary wooden buildings were erected at the Infirmary to accommodate the expected high numbers of casualties. They were sufficiently substantial that they are still in use today. In one incident early in the war, people hearing the sound of planes looked up expecting to watch planes from the RAF base at Grangemouth carrying out training manoeuvres and were startled to see the Iron Cross of the Luftwaffe on the first plane, followed by an RAF fighter. Falkirk was spared the blitz but some bombs did fall in the area, dropped by bombers returning from the devastating raids on Clydeside. Money was raised for the war effort through war bonds and special funds such as for the purchase of a Spitfire fighter. The plane was presented to the RAF in 1941 and was named 'The Falkirk Bairn'. As elsewhere, iron railings and decorative ironwork were cut down for use as scrap. No doubt some Bairns were sorry to see work they had helped produce disappear. There was less demand for cast iron in this war, but

Carron Company produced steel shells - on machinery installed in 1938 by German engineers. Grange foundry in Camelon and Callendar foundry produced hand grenades. R & A Main's Gothic foundry in Camelon made tail sections for Spitfires - using Irish linen cured with dope rather than cast iron. Those too old to be called up or in reserved occupations joined the Home Guard, became ARP (Air Raid Precautions) wardens or Special Constables. Initially the Falkirk battalion of the Home Guard was armed with two borrowed shotguns, but by the end of the war they had a range of effective weaponry. Women were conscripted too into the WAAF or WRENS or sent to work on the land or in factories, sometimes locally but also far away to new factories in the south of England. Any spare ground was dug up to grow vegetables including at Falkirk High School where two pupils shared each plot. Children were not evacuated from Falkirk, but it was not thought safe enough to be a receiving area. However, evacuees from Clydeside passed through its stations on their way to outlying villages.

Falkirk played host, not to American GIs but to the Free Polish Army in exile, its officers taking over Callander House and the men being accommodated in the three-storey building in East Bridge Street. Pupils at Victoria Park Primary School learned the Polish national anthem and sang it to the troops to make them feel more at home. Many chose to settle here after the war as the Polish Ex-Servicemen's Club in Arnot Street bears witness.

MAIN STREET, CAMELON, AFTER THE LIFTING OF THE TRAMLINES 1939
SA000469 (Courtesy of University of St Andrews Library)

THE PLAQUE ON THE DOOR OF THE POLISH EX-SERVICEMEN'S CLUB 2005 ZZZ05078 (David Elliot)

decorated and floodlit. Victory dances were held at the ice rink, at Turpie's and at Doak's Palais de Dance. In May 2005, the Royal Signal Core chose Falkirk to celebrate the 60th anniversary, ensuring that the sacrifices made were not forgotten by later generations.

A STORY OF THE WAR

An old farming couple called Buchanan lived in a cottage with a corrugated iron roof near the River Carron. The ground round about was soft, and when a German plane returning in the middle of the night from the Blitz on Clydebank dropped a stick of bombs, the mud flew in the air and clattered down on the iron roof of the cottage. The old woman lying in bed next to her husband turned to him and told him 'tae get they coos aff the roof'.

This time the Argylls raised only nine battalions and the local loss of life was thankfully less than in the previous conflict. Nonetheless, the new plaque on the cenotaph in Dollar Park recorded 'On the sea, in earth's distant places or at home, and in the air, nearly 220 men and women of Falkirk died for their country in the cause of Righteousness. 1939-1945.'

VE Day (Victory in Europe Day) was celebrated over several days. A victory bonfire was lit in Princes Park and the Burgh Buildings in Newmarket Street were

In the 1950s and 60s, a new spate of council house building took place, the most eye-catching being the high flats in Callendar Park and elsewhere. Unlike in many towns and cities, they have been a success. Also in the 1960s, the council built a new town hall and municipal buildings, in West Bridge Street. Although many mourned the loss of the old town hall, the new one has kept on the tradition of diverse and attractive entertainments.

TWO FALKIRK CHARACTERS

King Kenny was a tall, educated man, but he became a bit boisterous when he had been drinking. In the late 1940s he entertained the queues outside the Salon cinema on Saturday nights by playing the ukulele, drawing caricatures on the pavement and telling jokes and stories. He could even recite the Gettysburg Address. He used to claim that unlike most people he had a certificate to prove that he was sane - issued by Bellsdyke hospital.

In contrast, George Bottleman Washington was a wee chap. He earned money by collecting returnable bottles. The children must have thought he was the Pied Piper, as they would follow him up the street. George would stop and give them a Bible lesson.

CALLENDAR HOUSE AS A VISITOR ATTRACTION

The Council placed a compulsory purchase order on Callendar estates. Hence after centuries in which the inhabitants of Callendar House exercised control over the people of Falkirk, the roles were reversed. The Forbes left their family home. For years it sat boarded up, at risk from fire-raisers, and one councillor even suggested its demolition. Thankfully it survived, and has now become a visitor attraction telling the story of the house, the town and district. Interesting features include the shops and kitchen set in the 1820s. It is a working kitchen with a blazing fire. You can watch and taste the cooking and baking.

As part of a wartime programme to disperse vital industries, an aluminium rolling mill to produce sheeting for aircraft construction was built at David's Loan in Bainsford. Under British Aluminium and then Alcan it was to become an important part of Falkirk's industrial base for 60 years, employing 2,000 at one point. The employment was needed, because the post-war housing boom did not bring work to the foundries in the way it had after the First World War. One by one the great foundries closed as the market for light castings was lost to new materials, and cheap imports ate into what was left. From the 1950s a sad litany of closures ensued: Callendar and Callendar Abbots; Carmuirs in 1968; Camelon and Mungal in 1976; Etna, Forth and Clyde, R and A Main's Gothic Works, Grange, Cockburns, then the shattering blows of the Falkirk Iron Works in 1981 and Carron Company itself in 1982, Merchiston, Bainsford, and the last big company, the Grahamston, in 1994. Companies in associated industries, such as firebrick manufacturers Towers and Stein, eventually followed. Surprisingly little of the physical legacy remains - the odd factory shed now re-used for other purposes. The great Carron Company offices were demolished for the sake of a car park, leaving the clock spire looking slightly ridiculous. To the great credit of Carron Phoenix, a company born out of the ashes of Carron, the magnificent Grahamston Iron Company gates have been restored, although you have to go to the company entrance off the old Carron Road to see them.

However, the true physical legacy of Falkirk's iron founding days lies in its products, many still in daily use, and spotting them can be addictive. For some poor souls, including the author, it is impossible to pass a pillar box, old-style phone box, country house kitchen range, cannon or even drain cover, without discreetly looking to see if it came from one of

Falkirk's great companies. All over the world, in streets, houses and forts, and at the bottom of the sea in the galleys of sunken ships, rest the products of this once great industry.

The drinks industry fared no better. Firstly Aitken's Brewery, having become part of Tennent Caledonian, was closed in 1966 and the site redeveloped for a supermarket (now Asda) and car parking. Then in 1990s Rosebank Distillery ceased distilling, the buildings being converted into a restaurant and flats. Bottles of its fine product now attract high prices. And lastly, A G Barrs of Irn Bru fame, having moved in 1971 to a new factory at Port Downie, to the irritation of

A DRAIN COVER BY THE GRAHAMSTON IRON COMPANY 2005 ZZZ05079 (David Elliot)

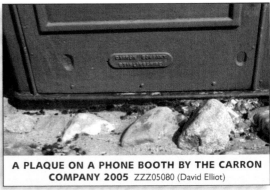

A PLAQUE ON A PHONE BOOTH BY THE CARRON COMPANY 2005 ZZZ05080 (David Elliot)

A PILLAR BOX BY THE CARRON COMPANY 2005 ZZZ05081 (David Elliot)

many Bairns, left the town in the 1990s for yet larger premises in Cumbernauld.

In 1962, the Forth and Clyde Canal was closed to navigation. Fisherman and yachtsmen were still using it, but roads were being expanded and it was cheaper to fill in the canal than to build a bridge over it. Although the campaign to re-open the canal started not long afterwards, for 40 years it was left to moulder away, the lock arms cut off and the channel weed-infested.

By the 1980s, the town was in a sorry state with derelict sites in abundance. The High Street was unattractive and choked with traffic. Unemployment rose and with the closure of the Falkirk Iron Company, the mighty Carron, and Grahamston, marking the demise of the industry that had sustained the town for so long, the town was in danger of losing its pride and self-respect. Fortunately, continuing expansion at the Grangemouth petro-chemical complex provided new job opportunities and the council parks department, surely one of the best in the land, did its bit by its colourful floral displays, which brought success in the Scotland in Bloom and Britain in Bloom contests.

Things began to look up for the town when, after years of delay, the Howgate Centre opened to rival the Thistle Centre in Stirling. At the east end of the High Street, Callendar Riggs shopping centre, a piece of brutalist 1960s architecture, was demolished in 1989, and after a two-year halt in its construction, the new Callendar shopping centre opened in 1993. Its cupola greets the visitor approaching from the east and mirrors similar features on older buildings at the top of Lint Riggs and Vicar Street. At the other end of the town, Camelon received a new health centre, the Mariner leisure centre with pool and squash courts, and a ten-pin bowling alley. The old Falkirk book-binding firm of Dunn & Wilson, and Johnston's presses re-located there too. The 1990s saw a welcome return to traditional building materials of stone and harling, in harmony with Falkirk's past. First adopted for public buildings such as the new Falkirk sheriff court, built with red sandstone and marble, most private developers of houses and flats have returned to these materials so much more in keeping with the townscape than brick. Unfortunately there are still some private houses being built which would look more at home in the south of England than in Falkirk.

As the century ended one construction project stood out over all others in terms of interest and anticipation: the project to re-open the Forth and Clyde and Union Canals to navigation. There were grounds to believe that the future once more looked promising.

A ROUNDABOUT ON CALLENDAR ROAD 2005
ZZZ05094 (David Elliot)

Falkirk Council's roundabouts are truly remarkable. There is even one representing a beach in the West Highlands.

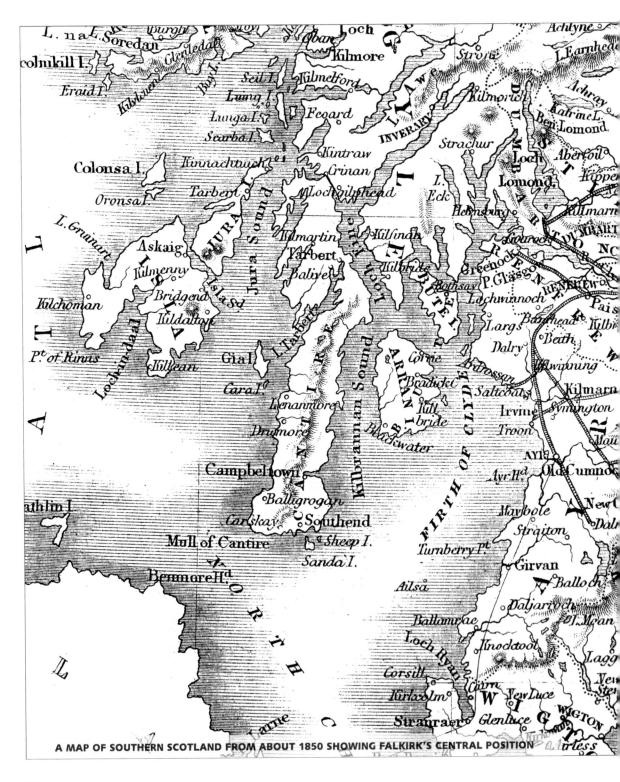

A MAP OF SOUTHERN SCOTLAND FROM ABOUT 1850 SHOWING FALKIRK'S CENTRAL POSITION

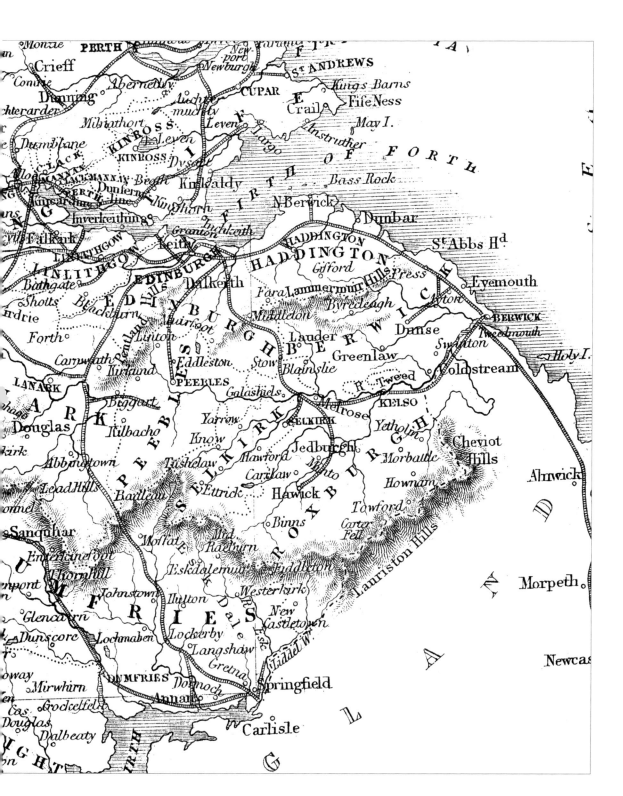

CHAPTER FIVE

THE PHOENIX ARISES

THE CANAL RE-OPENS, CAMELON 2001 F248708k (Alex Burt)

WITH THE COMING of the new millennium, Falkirk acquired the Falkirk Wheel and a new symbol. It is a worthy addition to the two iconic buildings, the Old Parish Kirk and the Steeple. The Millennium Link project of which the Wheel is part re-opened the Union and Forth and Clyde Canals at a cost of £84.5 million.

THE FALKIRK WHEEL 2005 F248709k (David Elliot)

The Falkirk Wheel was the ingenious solution to a major problem facing the engineers. The 11 locks which had once joined the Union Canal to Port Downie and the Forth and Clyde Canal were buried in the 1930s and built over. Some new way of linking the two canals had to be found, one that would be much faster than the old locks.

The innovative solution was a rotating boat lift, the only one of its kind in the world. It was built to the west of the original locks, at Tamfourhill. This required an extension to the canal running parallel to the railway and then turning at right angles under it, and the construction of the 145 metre long Rough Castle tunnel to take it under the Antonine Wall. From the exit of the tunnel the canal seems to vanish into space at the top of the 35 metre high wheel.

THE CANAL IN THE SKY 2005 F248710k (David Elliot)

A new canal basin was built, called New Port Downie.

The wheel has two gondolas, each holding 300 tonnes of water. It can take up to eight boats at a time. The gondolas are always in perfect balance, because boats displace their own weight in water, so it doesn't matter how many boats are in each gondola. It is so finely balanced that it takes only 1.5 kilowatts of electrical power to rotate the wheel. The old locks took nearly all day to negotiate and used up 3,500 tons of water. The wheel takes 15 minutes and doesn't use any water. It is now one of the most popular visitor attractions in Scotland, and was visited by 400,000 people in 2004.

THE GONDOLAS IN PERFECT BALANCE 2005
F248711k (David Elliot)

At the other end of the town another structure in gleaming metal has been constructed. Falkirk Football Club first planned to quit Brockville not long after the First World War; but it eventually happened

THE VISITOR CENTRE AND NEW PORT DOWNIE 2005 F24871 2k (David Elliot)

in 2003. The stadium now boasts a west and north stand and meets the Premier League's requirement for 6,000 seats.

Many of the schools have moved into new buildings, such as Graeme High School on the eastern approach to the town. Plans are being made to provide Falkirk High and St Mungo's with new buildings by 2008. The fire station has been replaced, as has the police station - by a substantial building faced in stone on the same site on West Bridge Street. The number of pubs in the town centre is probably no more than in the past, but many of them are much bigger than before and are more oriented to food and entertainment than the drinking dens of previous centuries.

Falkirk's enduring love of the cinema is well catered for in the Cineworld multiplex and during a week in which a blockbuster is screened, some 20,000 people pass through its doors.

Falkirk town centre is thriving, according to Alistair Mitchell, the town centre manager. The Howgate and Central Retail Park attract nine million visitors each year and Callendar Square six million. The town's attraction is the mix of chain stores, family-run shops and the 'intown out-of-town' retail park. The High Street is now the longest uninterrupted pedestrianised street in Scotland and some of its historic atmosphere has been brought back by the farmers' market and French markets

FALKIRK FC PROMOTED TO THE SPL!

Falkirk Football Club has been through the mill since being relegated from the Premier Division back in 1996. However, that was all in the past as the club went into the 2005-6 season in the Scottish Premier League, playing at its newly extended stadium. The club benefits from the town's sense of identity, meaning most football supporters identify with their town's main team. But the club wants to win Falkirk hearts and minds. One way, according to George Craig, Commercial Manager and a Bairn himself, is through one of the most inclusive and diverse community programmes in Scottish football. By offering football coaching to young boys and girls, and indeed to all ages and abilities, the club hopes to ensure that the coming generations get behind Falkirk Football Club. With the combination of a new stadium, accessibility and Premier League football, the club is well placed to compete for supporters with the likes of the Old Firm.

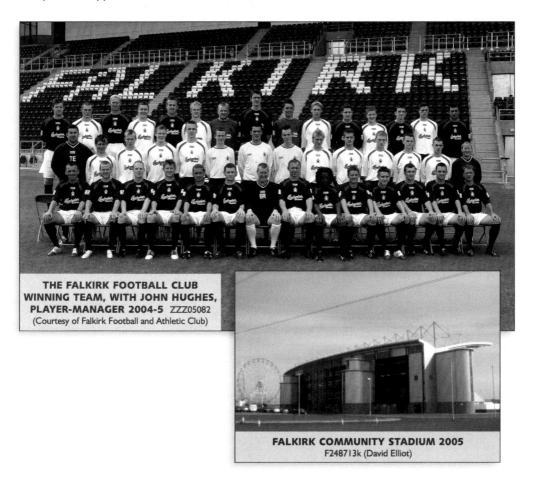

THE FALKIRK FOOTBALL CLUB WINNING TEAM, WITH JOHN HUGHES, PLAYER-MANAGER 2004-5 ZZZ05082
(Courtesy of Falkirk Football and Athletic Club)

FALKIRK COMMUNITY STADIUM 2005
F248713k (David Elliot)

THE NEW GRAEME HIGH SCHOOL BUILDING 2005 F248715k (David Elliot)

THE FRENCH STREET MARKET 2005 F248714k (David Elliot)

held there. Perhaps it is time to pedestrianise Manor Street too. The combination of shopping malls and small shops has led Falkirk to be rated the top town in Scotland in overall retail spending, after the four main cities and Inverness.

AN ADVERTISEMENT FOR THE CONTINENTAL MARKET 2003 ZZZ05083
(Courtesy of Falkirk Town Centre Management)

The loss of manufacturing jobs continued with the closure of the Alcan aluminium plant, but there were also successes. Carron Phoenix is well named, having risen from the ashes of the great Carron Company. The rescue in May 2004 of the bus-building works in Camelon by three prominent Scottish

FALKIRK'S LONG-ESTABLISHED FAMILY SHOPS

MOSCARDINI BROTHERS 2005
ZZZ05090 (David Elliot)

A surprising number of Falkirk shops have been in business for many years. Thomas Johnston the butchers was established in 1861, at one time occupying the ground floor of the Steeple. Mathieson's the bakers, now moving to a big new bakery, dates from 1872. We have to thank Italian migration for Moscardini Brothers' period-piece fish restaurant in Manor Street (1880s), the Lamettis of Camelon (1895), the Serafinis (the York Café) and Cascis. McCalls of Falkirk dates from 1887. Malley's bicycle shop in Grahamston was founded in 1890 on the same site as today and G W Smith's in the High Street can trace its origins to 1897. Miss Forsyth's (corset and underclothing specialist) in Lint Riggs is over a century old and Miss Grant's the milliners and Taylor's furniture store date from the 1920s. James Sime, a qualified saw doctor, was supplying tools back in 1878 and the shop has been in Cow Wynd since 1922. Even Leckie's, 'the Harrod's of Falkirk', has been around since 1961.

businessmen has given the company a new lease of life under the name of Alexander Dennis. It now employs about 800 workers and is one of Europe's major bus builders. Falkirk-built buses carry over 10 million passengers a day in London and Hong Kong. Grangemouth continues to provide many Falkirk workers with employment even if the names of the companies change. The dispersal of civil service jobs has helped, with the Child Support Agency and the Office of the Public Guardian now located in Callendar business park. In 2005 the Forth Valley Sensory Centre opened in Camelon. A new acute hospital is to be opened in 2009 at Bellsdyke Road and possibly a community hospital on the site of Falkirk Royal Infirmary in 2010.

Falkirk College was Scotland's fifth largest, with 17,500 students, most of whom were part-time. It has now merged with Clackmannan College to form the even larger Forth Valley College.

As Maureen Campbell of Falkirk Council points out, there are few areas with two international airports within 35 minutes, six trains an hour to the two major cities and easy access to the motorway network, a seaport, and a rail freight distribution centre. It should bode well for economic growth. A new phenomenon that would surprise previous generations of Bairns is the growth of Falkirk as a commuting town. While the population of the town itself has stabilised at around 35,000 (Bainsford, Camelon and Laurieston included), the council has allocated land for up to 14,000 new houses in the wider area. One benefit of commuting is

that the town is no longer wholly dependent on a few local industries.

Looking further ahead, it is hoped that the Falkirk Gateway and the 'My Future's in Falkirk' projects will create 3,000 permanent jobs on a 300-acre site, through a mixture of business space, a retail park, a hotel and conference facilities and a new marina linked to the Forth and Clyde Canal. Next to it will be an 'urban country park'. Nothing can be guaranteed, but, if the estate agent adage of 'location, location, location' is even half true, then Falkirk should succeed.

On the cultural side, the number of organisations operating in Falkirk is too long to list here. Big in Falkirk, with its mixture of events, attracts over 100,000 visitors each year. The Falkirk Tryst Festival, celebrating drama, music and art has now been running for 40 years. Mariner's Day is gala day in Camelon. There is the Youth Theatre, the long-established Falkirk Operatic Society, and Falkirk Bohemians. There are many charities, for example Bairns Aid, which has a long-term commitment to an area of Sri Lanka devastated by the tsunami.

BIG IN FALKIRK 2005 F248716k (David Elliot)

The Antonine Wall is being put forward as a World Heritage site, in collaboration with Germany, Austria and Hungary to mark the European boundary of the Roman Empire.

A thousand years ago the monks at Holyrood told the early citizens of Falkirk what to do, and took their surplus food off to Edinburgh. Holyrood again plays a big part in the life of Falkirk, but this time it is neither the abbey nor the palace, but the re-convened Scottish parliament. At least now the Bairns can send politicians there to speak up for them, and vote them out if they don't. It is in line with Falkirk's past that one of its representatives, unselected by his party, should be elected and re-elected as an Independent, reflecting the old motto better meddle wi the deil…

The town in earlier times endured war, plague and weak town government. It also enjoyed in the 19th and 20th centuries considerable wealth arising from the Tryst and the dynamic iron-founding industry. The physical legacy is to be seen in Falkirk's many fine public buildings and houses. Over the years, life for the Bairns has never been easy or tranquil. But out of adversity has grown the vigorous town of today, proud of its past and focussed on the future.

ONE OF THE LOCAL ENTERTAINERS AT BIG IN FALKIRK 2005 ZZZ05084 (David Elliot)

CALLENDAR HOUSE TODAY - FALKIRK'S CHATEAU 2005 F248717k (David Elliot)

ACKNOWLEDGEMENTS

My thanks to former colleagues at Callendar House, especially Geoff Bailey for reading and commenting on the draft, Carol Sneddon, for her suggestions for additional material, and the archive staff, Elspeth Reid and Maria Castrillo, for welcoming me back. I am grateful to Falkirk Council and Lewis Lawson for permission to draw on his pioneering 'History of Falkirk'. 30 years after publication, it is still well worth reading, as is Ian Scott's 'Life and Times', published in 1994. I have also found 'Calatria' an invaluable source and acknowledge my debt to those who have written articles for it. Thanks also to George Craig of Falkirk Football Club; Clare McNair of the British Waterways Board, Scotland; Alistair Mitchell, Town Centre Manager and Ian White and Stewart Cameron of Falkirk Council. Thanks also to Isobel for listening. My special thanks go to all those Bairns, too many to name, who gave of their time to talk about Falkirk's past. Their warmth and enthusiasm made the research a real pleasure. Any mistakes, however, are mine.

The author and publisher gratefully acknowledge the use of material from the collections of Falkirk Council Cultural Services. Copies of many of the photographs in the collections may be purchased from Falkirk Council Archives, Callendar House, Callendar Park, Falkirk FK1 1YR. Photographs from the Falkirk Herald Collection at Falkirk Council Archives are used by courtesy of the Falkirk Herald.

Photographs used by courtesy of University of St Andrews Library are reproduced from digital copies of the originals held in the University of St Andrews Library. For further information about the collections, obtaining copies of images, or authorisation to reproduce them, please refer to http://specialcollections.st-and.ac.uk or contact Department of Special Collections, University of St Andrews Library, North Street, St Andrews, Fife KY16 9TR (tel 01334-462339); email speccoll@st-and.ac.uk

ACKNOWLEDGEMENTS & BIBLIOGRAPHY

FURTHER READING LIST

Geoff B Bailey: 'Falkirk or Paradise! The Battle of Falkirk Muir, 17 January 1746', John Donald Publishers Ltd, Edinburgh, 1996

Geoff B Bailey: 'Falkirk 400', Falkirk Council, Falkirk, 2000.

Geoff B Bailey: 'The Antonine Wall: Rome's Northern Frontier', Falkirk Council, Falkirk, 2003

Alan W Brotchie: 'The Tramways of Falkirk', published by the NB Traction Group, 1975

Calatria, The Journal of the Falkirk Local History Society, Numbers 1 to 21, Falkirk, 1991-2005

John Dickson: 'Heroes Departed. Falkirk District during the First World War', Falkirk District Council Libraries, Falkirk

John Dickson et al: 'Travelling Through Time: Travelling in the Falkirk District', Falkirk District Council Libraries, Falkirk, 1993

T J Dowds: 'The Forth and Clyde Canal: A History', Tuckwell Press, East Linton, East Lothian, 2003

A R B Haldane: 'The Drove Roads of Scotland', House of Lochar, Isle of Colonsay, Argyll, 1995. First published 1952

Guthrie Hutton: 'A Forth and Clyde Canalbum', Richard Stenlake Publishing, 1991

Guthrie Hutton: 'The Union Canal: a Capital Asset', Richard Stenlake Publishing, 1993

Guthrie Hutton: 'Old Falkirk', Richard Stenlake Publishing, 1995

Lewis Lawson: 'A History of Falkirk', Falkirk Town Council, Falkirk, 1975

Don Martin and A A Maclean: 'Edinburgh & Glasgow Railway Guidebook', Strathkelvin District Libraries and Museum, Bishopbriggs, 1992.

Old Statistical Account, 1799 and New Statistical Account, 1845

Ian Scott: 'The Life and Times of Falkirk', John Donald Publishers, Edinburgh, 1994

Brian Watters: 'Where Iron Runs Like Water! A New History of the Carron Iron Works 1759-1982', John Donald Publishers, Edinburgh, 1998

FRITH PRODUCTS & SERVICES

Francis Frith would doubtless be pleased to know that the pioneering publishing venture he started in 1860 still continues today. Over a hundred and forty years later, The Francis Frith Collection continues in the same innovative tradition and is now one of the foremost publishers of vintage photographs in the world. Some of the current activities include:

INTERIOR DECORATION

Today Frith's photographs can be seen framed and as giant wall murals in thousands of pubs, restaurants, hotels, banks, retail stores and other public buildings throughout the country. In every case they enhance the unique local atmosphere of the places they depict and provide reminders of gentler days in an increasingly busy and frenetic world.

PRODUCT PROMOTIONS

Frith products are used by many major companies to promote the sales of their own products or to reinforce their own history and heritage. Frith promotions have been used by Hovis bread, Courage beers, Scots Porage Oats, Colman's mustard, Cadbury's foods, Mellow Birds coffee, Dunhill pipe tobacco, Guinness, and Bulmer's Cider.

GENEALOGY AND FAMILY HISTORY

As the interest in family history and roots grows world-wide, more and more people are turning to Frith's photographs of Great Britain for images of the towns, villages and streets where their ancestors lived; and, of course, photographs of the churches and chapels where their ancestors were christened, married and buried are an essential part of every genealogy tree and family album.

FRITH PRODUCTS

All Frith photographs are available Framed or just as Mounted Prints and Posters (size 23 x 16 inches). These may be ordered from the address below. Other products available are - Address Books, Calendars, Jigsaws, Canvas Prints, Postcards and local and prestige books.

THE INTERNET

Already ninety thousand Frith photographs can be viewed and purchased on the internet through the Frith websites and a myriad of partner sites.

For more detailed information on Frith products, look at this site:
www.francisfrith.com

See the complete list of Frith Books at: www.francisfrith.com
This web site is regularly updated with the latest list of publications from The Francis Frith Collection. If you wish to buy books relating to another part of the country that your local bookshop does not stock, you may purchase on-line.

For further information, trade, or author enquiries please contact us at the address below:
The Francis Frith Collection, Unit 6, Oakley Business Park, Wylye Road, Dinton, Wiltshire SP3 5EU.
Tel: +44 (0)1722 716 376 Fax: +44 (0)1722 716 881 Email: sales@francisfrith.co.uk

See Frith products on the internet at www.francisfrith.com

FREE PRINT OF YOUR CHOICE

Mounted Print
Overall size 14 x 11 inches (355 x 280mm)

Choose any Frith photograph in this book.
Simply complete the Voucher opposite and return it with your remittance for £3.50 (to cover postage and handling) and we will print the photograph of your choice in SEPIA (size 11 x 8 inches) and supply it in a cream mount with a burgundy rule line (overall size 14 x 11 inches).
Please note: aerial photographs and photographs with a reference number starting with a "Z" are not Frith photographs and cannot be supplied under this offer. Offer valid for delivery to one UK address only.

PLUS: Order additional Mounted Prints at HALF PRICE - £9.50 each (normally £19.00)
If you would like to order more Frith prints from this book, possibly as gifts for friends and family, you can buy them at half price (with no additional postage and handling costs).

PLUS: Have your Mounted Prints framed
For an extra £18.00 per print you can have your mounted print(s) framed in an elegant polished wood and gilt moulding, overall size 16 x 13 inches (no additional postage and handling required).

IMPORTANT!

These special prices are only available if you use this form to order. You must use the ORIGINAL VOUCHER on this page (no copies permitted). We can only despatch to one UK address. This offer cannot be combined with any other offer.

Send completed Voucher form to:
The Francis Frith Collection, Unit 6, Oakley Business Park, Wylye Road, Dinton, Wiltshire SP3 5EU

CHOOSE A PHOTOGRAPH FROM THIS BOOK

Voucher *for* **FREE** *and Reduced Price Frith Prints*

Please do not photocopy this voucher. Only the original is valid, so please fill it in, cut it out and return it to us with your order.

Picture ref no	Page no	Qty	Mounted @ £9.50	Framed + £18.00	Total Cost £
		1	Free of charge*	£	£
			£9.50	£	£
			£9.50	£	£
			£9.50	£	£
			£9.50	£	£
			£9.50	£	£

Please allow 28 days for delivery.
Offer available to one UK address only

* Post & handling   £3.50

Total Order Cost   £

Title of this book . . . .

I enclose a cheque/postal order for £ . . . .
made payable to 'The Francis Frith Collection'

OR please debit my Mastercard / Visa / Maestro card, details below

Card Number:

Issue No (Maestro only):   Valid from (Maestro):

Card Security Number: Expires:

Signature:

Name Mr/Mrs/Ms . . . .

Address . . . .

. . . .

. . . .

. . . . Postcode . . . .

Daytime Tel No . . . .

Email . . . .

Valid to 31/12/12

Can you help us with information about any of the Frith photographs in this book?

We are gradually compiling an historical record for each of the photographs in the Frith archive. It is always fascinating to find out the names of the people shown in the pictures, as well as insights into the shops, buildings and other features depicted.

If you recognize anyone in the photographs in this book, or if you have information not already included in the author's caption, do let us know. We would love to hear from you, and will try to publish it in future books or articles.

An Invitation from The Francis Frith Collection to Share Your Memories

The 'Share Your Memories' feature of our website allows members of the public to add personal memories relating to the places featured in our photographs, or comment on others already added. Seeing a place from your past can rekindle forgotten or long held memories. Why not visit the website, find photographs of places you know well and add YOUR story for others to read and enjoy? We would love to hear from you!

www.francisfrith.com/memories

Our production team

Frith books are produced by a small dedicated team at offices near Salisbury. Most have worked with the Frith Collection for many years. All have in common one quality: they have a passion for the Frith Collection.

Frith Books and Gifts

We have a wide range of books and gifts available on our website utilising our photographic archive, many of which can be individually personalised.

www.francisfrith.com